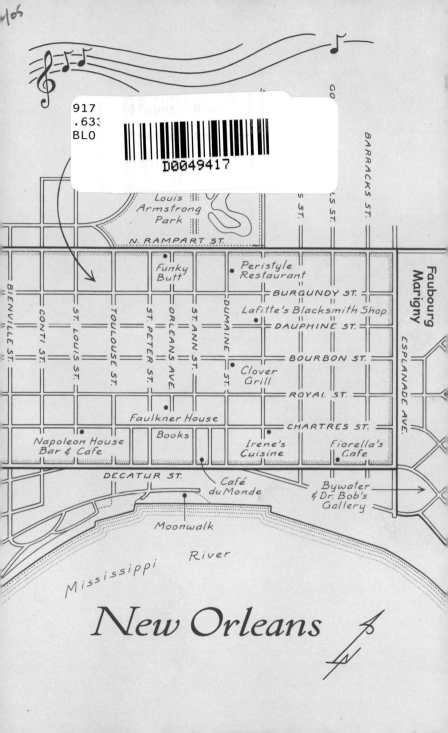

Feet on the Street

ALSO BY ROY BLOUNT JR.

Feet on the Street

RAMBLES AROUND
NEW ORLEANS

Roy Blount Jr.

CROWN JOURNEYS

CROWN PUBLISHERS · NEW YORK

For Joan, in New Orleans and all over

CROWN JOURNEYS *and the Crown Journeys colophon are trademarks of*
Random House, Inc.

Library of Congress Cataloging-in-Publication Data

Blount, Roy.
   Feet on the street: rambles around New Orleans/Roy Blount Jr.
     (Crown journeys)
1. New Orleans (La.)—Description and travel.   2. New Orleans
(La.)—Social life and customs.   3. New Orleans (La.)—Biography.
4. Walking—Louisiana—New Orleans.   5. Blount, Roy—Travel—
Louisiana—New Orleans.   I. Title.   II. Crown Journeys series
   F379.N54B58   2005
   917.63'35—dc22   *2004021471*

ISBN 1-4000-4645-9

Printed in the United States of America

Design by Lauren Dong
Map by Jackie Aher

10 9 8 7 6 5 4 3 2 1

First Edition

Contents

INTRODUCTION

*. . . the low city . . . the labyrinthine mass of oleander
and jasmine, lantana and mimosa . . .*

—WILLIAM FAULKNER, *Absalom, Absalom!*

They say anything will grow here, and everything eats it.

—A LONG-TIME RESIDENT

THIS DOESN'T LOOK LIKE AN AMERICAN STREET.
It's lined with architecture, some of it rotting, some
of it in the dusty process of preservation; a variety of styles
but largely late-eighteenth-century-to-mid-nineteenth-
century Spanish-influence, because nearly all the original
wooden French buildings burned in 1788 and 1794,
while the city was under Spanish rule, and were replaced
with stuccoed tiled-roof brick structures with lacy ironwork and—oh look, there's somebody out on one of the

balconies now, smashing windows with a champagne bottle. "That's all right," explains a passing stranger who notes our concern, "it's her place. She's having some little problems with her family life." Chameleons skitter across turquoise stucco to disappear among elephant-ear leaves and bougainvillea blossoms, which Tennessee Williams likened to bloodshot eyes.

A sign says the street is a "Calle," which is Spanish. Back home what we're walking on would be the sidewalk, but here it's the banquette, an old Creole word, pronounced *bang*-kit, from the French for a raised walk around a parapet. The history is so thick around here you could pop it open with an oyster-knife, and oh, the aromarama: fresh-ground coffee, spilt beer, hot pastry, sloshed Tabasco, yesterday's fish, patchouli oil, and hints of some fortuitous compound . . . mule plop and olive salad?

We will not be starting off this day with alligator sausage, because the Tally Ho Café, on Chartres (pronounced Charters), has closed, having been run into by a car. So we have had a light, open-air breakfast of sugar-dusted beignets and a small chickory-flavored coffee at the Café du Monde on Decatur, while enjoying the day's rich harvest of obituaries in the daily *Times-Picayune*: only one due-to-gunshot-wound, which is unusual, but many great-named persons are mentioned, including the late Theoclecia Bijou Bourgeois, the late Glideville Creech, two different men named Dermis, a "Honey Bunny," a Charmyra, a J'John, and three different women given-named Marie Antoinette, one of whom married a Champagne. Providing musical accompaniment to breakfast was Jack the boombox man, standing in the street in red shorts and tube socks, playing the Beach Boys. Some days he plays gospel, some days jazz, whatever he has a mind to play. Once he was playing Sinatra reeealll sloowww, and my friend Rosemary James handed him some new batteries, which he took under advisement. Jack isn't selling anything, this is just how he chooses to spend his afternoon. He is a character.

Yes, afternoon. We are off to what might somewhere else be considered a late start, because last night after smoked softshell crab and grilled baby drum at Clancy's, on Annunciation, we did some dancing to the ReBirth Brass Band at the Maple Leaf club uptown, where the crowd sweated and swole and spilled out onto the street, and from there we went to the Saturn Bar over on St. Claude, whose beyond-grungy décor incorporates a Greek frieze, lots of red and white and yellow neon chandeliers, a psychedelic painting of a dragon, several pairs of panties, and a bumper sticker that says I'D RATHER BE AT THE OPERA. That must have been where we listened to a man with a crucifix hand-painted on his hat tell us about his father, who accumulated lots of cars in his yard and every Saturday would take his one battery around to each car and crank it. Because it was later, while we were having that nightcap at the Napoleon House, which is over two hundred years old, that the young couple in evening wear came in, looking

pale, and swore that they had just seen the ghost of a beautiful naked quadroon lady humming a melody that they
could not for the life of them recall.

And now, cutting through the clip-clop of the mules
drawing carriages over the cobblestones, we hear:

> *Betcha I can tell ya*
> *Where ya*
> *Got them shoooes.*

African-American lad about nine years old. Doing a
lickety-clackety shuffle on flattened halves of Fresca cans af-
fixed to his sneaker soles.

"Don't want to take advantage of you, young man.
How could you possibly know—"

> *Betchadollar,*
> *Betchadollar,*
> *Where ya*
> *Got them shoooes.*

"Well, all right . . ." We show our dollar, and the lad,
clickle-lickity clack, delivers:

> *Got your shoes on your feet,*
> *Got your feet on the street,*
> *And the street's in Noo*
> *Awlins, Loo-*
> *Eez-ee-anna.*

Where I, for my part, first ate a live oyster, and first saw a naked woman with the lights on. I was startled by both, they both by me—presumably in the first case, regrettably in the second. Where I first heard the blues, first met an eminent author, or any other kind of author, and first realized that a person of my own gender could have designs (when I was much younger) on my, uh, body. Every time I go to New Orleans I am startled by something.

NEW ORLEANS IS nobody's oyster. It is situated, however, like a served-up oyster—the half-shell being the levees that keep Lake Pontchartrain and the Mississippi River from engulfing the city. New Orleans lies several feet below river and lake level, and it sinks a little farther every year. When the big hurricane hits—and it will, New Orleanians assure you, with what suffices locally for civic pride—the waters will finally rise over the shell and inundate the town, killing tens of thousands.

Here is one thing you hear, locally, about the flood: "It hasn't happened yet. That proves that we're blessed."

Here is another: "I hope it won't, but if it does I'd hate to miss it."

And another: "The other morning, I woke up thinking it happened last night."

Many New Orleanians, in what suffices locally for prudence, have taken the precaution, officially urged by what suffices locally for civil authority, of keeping an ax in the attic. So they can chop a hole up through the roof, when the time comes, and rise above the flood.

There will be rooftop parties. Neither pestilence nor fire nor corruption nor rioting nor thuggery nor a series of governing powers—French then Spanish then French again then American then Confederate then American again—has managed to dampen New Orleanian spirits for long, so why should the Deluge?

"One day it's coming," I heard that expert say on the news, and when it does, "it's very probable that the French Quarter becomes one massive tomb."

But then New Orleanians don't get down in the mouth about death. Marching to a jazz funeral, a New Orleans band plays something slow and dirgey, but marching away it's upbeat: "Oh, Didn't He Ramble," a celebration of all that the deceased managed to get away with in his or her time.

New Orleans is my favorite place in the world to ramble. Even on those deep-summer days that make a person feel swathed in slowly melting hamfat, New Orleans has always put a spring in my step. Trying to do New Orleans justice, however, makes me feel like Audra MacDonald's child.

I mention Audra MacDonald not because she has anything to do with New Orleans music—her blues is too classical—but because of what I heard her say once in Carnegie Hall between songs: "My baby hates my voice.

As soon as I start singing to her, she bursts into tears." Well, put yourself in that baby's place. Out comes that rich histrionic lyric soprano and the child thinks, "Oh, Lord, couldn't you just be a regular mama? I'm not that great a baby!"

I can hear residents already: "He thinks he can write about N'woilins and never had a Nectar Cream with Cream [a sort of snow-cone] over by Hansen's or the cannibal salad—raw beef in it—at the Magnolia Grill? He thinks he can write about N'wawlin and never saw the Irish throwing cabbages from their St. Patrick's parade and the un-Irish picking them up to take home for supper? He thinks he can write about Noowawlins and can't even figure out how to spell how it's pronunciated right?" (The pronunciation *Noo Orleens* is just for song lyrics, rhyming as it does with *beans, means, queens,* and *scenes.*)

Residents do as residents will—they get into a particular Mardi Gras ball, a particular neighborhood, a particular bar, they develop little crotchets like claiming (oh, sure!) not to like beignets. They know what it means to miss the point of New Orleans. But here's something that New Orleanians tend to have in common: none of them believes that most of the others of them get New Orleans either. New Orleanian solidarity is a matter of *e pluribus falsibus unum:* from the erroneous many, one. Unless you have some kind of fetish about everybody pulling together, there is much to be said for this approach to truth.

Then too we could put it nicer. We could quote from

the legendary New Orleans musical figure Allen Toussaint. Toussaint's many achievements include writing "Workin' in the Coal Mine" with another legendary New Orleans musical figure, Lee Dorsey. In a radio interview with Harry Shearer, who is a part-time New Orleans resident, Toussaint said this about Dorsey:

"Lee was a body and fender man, you know, and a good one. When we were recording, there'd be his little glass of Chivas Regal with some of his grease on it. And a good dresser, when it was time to do that. Listening to Lee Dorsey you can see a smile. You could tell that he was very glad at all times to be at the moment where he was."

Toussaint said this about the great New Orleans funk band, the Meters: "From my own anatomy and ear and spinebone, the Meters were the most perfect group. The way the sparks were flying: that kind of syncopation that seems to be going in all directions, but there's a unity there."

Tourists may not catch this—those tourists who walk the tawdriest blocks of Bourbon Street, who see other tourists weaving along holding drinks known as hurricanes or flashing their breasts for trinkets, who eat in the wrong famous restaurants, and who go back home saying big deal like we never saw drunks or breasts or got overcharged before. They should have walked farther.

It is the person in between—me, the visitor who keeps coming back—who can give you some perspective. For one thing, if you happen to catch breasts-for-trinkets just right, it can be a breath of fresh air. (She flips up her top and out they pop, tender gamboling lambs, and she's flushed and she is cheered and gimcracks are thrown to her from a balcony and she and her friend go rambling off up the street to someplace where they can go over every inch of each other because they want to, bless their hearts. Though you can't help doubting that he's good enough for her.) Fresh air in New Orleans is like that kitten in *The Third Man,* the kitten who finds Harry Lime in the doorway, a great movie reveal mentioned by Walker Percy in *The Moviegoer.* It's fleeting, it's got to be a hardy damn kitten to be surviving in post–World War II Vienna, and it registers.

New Orleans is not what it once was, neither the fetid swamp nor the great city nor the readily affordable bohemia. Miami is now a more international town, Vegas more of a flesh-and-gambling mecca, and Memphis, thanks to FedEx, more of a hub. And if you know of a readily affordable bohemia in the United States today, I wish you'd tell me where. But New Orleans is still itself enough to erase any doubt that it *was* all the things it has been; it hasn't lost the feel. It's like no other place in America, and yet (or therefore) it's the cradle of American culture.

It's where Walt Whitman (he said) first tasted sin, where Abraham Lincoln got his first full sense of the scope and the primary shame of the nation, where Mark Twain began and ended his riverboat career and started imagining the books he would write, where Buddy Bolden and Bunk Johnson and Jelly Roll Morton became the first legends of jazz and Louis Armstrong put the "A" in American music, where W. C. Handy dreaded seeing that evening sun go down, where William Faulkner turned from poetry to fiction (and shot BBs at nuns from his garret window), where Huey Long went to law school, and where Tennessee Williams acquired his "Tennessee" and lost (he said) his virginity.

It's also where John James Audubon drew the whooping crane (working from a dead one brought by a hunter who shot it as it speared baby alligators with its beak) and put in several sessions painting a mysterious high-born lady naked, after she approached him in the street, wearing a veil, and asked him to meet her at a certain address.

Where Zora Neale Hurston got into voodoo, F. Scott Fitzgerald wrote *This Side of Paradise,* O. Henry took his pen name and refuge from the law, and Langston Hughes bought some Wishing Powder and "the next day, quite unexpectedly, I found myself on the way to Havana."

Where Kate Chopin smoked her first cigarette, Little Richard recorded "Good Golly, Miss Molly," the Boswell Sisters got their act together, Chuck Berry was inspired to write "Johnny B. Goode," Anita Loos wrote *Diamonds Are a Girl's Best Friend,* Ingrid Bergman (playing a trollop) ate jambalaya off the head of a dwarf, and a couple of guys tried to mug Richard Ford right out in front of his Garden District house but he didn't have any money on him so they got back in their car and drove away. Walker Percy and Robert Stone set their first novels here, in the sixties, Percy's lyrical-stoic, Stone's politico-phantasmagoric.

New Orleans is where Louis Prima, Lillian Hellman, Dorothy Lamour, Mahalia Jackson, George Herriman (creator of Krazy Kat), Doctor John, Madame X (portrayed scandalously off-the-shoulder in Paris by John Singer Sargent), Richard Simmons, Lloyd Price, Truman Capote, Elmore Leonard, and Lee Harvey Oswald were born, and where Randy Newman spent what he referred to in song as "my baby years." Where Walker Evans fell in love with the woman whom he would eventually marry but would first disappoint by leaving town when her husband brandished a gun at him. Where John Steinbeck and Hank Williams married their second wives (Hank, in response to popular demand, did it twice, on the same day, 3:00 p.m. and 7:00 p.m., in Municipal Auditorium, price of admission from $1.00 to $2.80). Where Jefferson Davis, in town for a visit, died. Where Gram Parsons and both Marie Laveaus are buried, and where Anne Rice, in a red wedding dress, popped up out of a closed coffin delivered by a horse-drawn hearse for a book-signing session.

In New Orleans, craps, café au lait, and the cocktail were invented, and the following were introduced to America: cocaine, tomato sauce, the free lunch, Marquis of Queensbury boxing, the term *arriviste,* and the Mafia. A New Orleanian's invention made sugar a common household item. The largest slave market in North America was here, and the first synagogue outside the original thirteen colonies. New Orleans was the first American city to build an opera house and the last to install a sewer system. It has been the most nearly European American city and the most nearly African. The northernmost Caribbean city and the westernmost Mediterranean. I know of two places where the *Marseillaise* was sung in defiance of an occupying power: Casablanca, in the movie, and New Orleans, under Union control.

I am not a New Orleans expert. If I'd lived here long enough to be that, I'd be dead, because New Orleans never closes. But then New Orleans has not generally been a place where creatives (see *lagniappe,* below), Fats Domino excepted, put down roots. It has been a place for reorientational interludes. Thomas Wolfe was here just long enough to muster the independence (or to intensify the paranoia) it took to sever his umbilical editorial connection to Maxwell Perkins. William Burroughs long enough, among "lamsters of every description," to get busted for possession and flee the country. Benito Juarez long enough to plot a revolution in Mexico, and Aaron Burr long enough to conspire to create a new empire with New Orleans as its capital. Edgar Degas long enough to be bowled over, visually, by all the black people around. Gertrude Stein long enough to find "New Orleans hot and delicious." Charles Bukowski to acknowledge that "being lost, being crazy maybe is not so bad if you can be that way undisturbed. New Orleans gave me that."

I spent one summer here, in 1963, working as a reporter at the *Times-Picayune* and living in a converted slave quarters, on St. Philip Street, around the corner from Lafitte's Blacksmith Shop. I was twenty-one and shy. I have returned, to the best of my recollection, thirty-eight times, for anywhere from two days to three weeks. I'll bet I have been up in N.O. at every hour in every season. It is not a town, in my experience, where a person takes meticulous notes, over the years, or keeps assiduous track of every note he does take. If this were school, I'd say the dog ate some of my research. But I can bring the dog to class and show you how fat he is and how apologetic he looks. (In 1922 Sherwood Anderson wrote, "When the fact is made secondary to the desire to live, to love, and to understand life, it may be that we will have in more American cities a charm of place such as one finds in the older parts of New Orleans now.") And I can take you to the river and on various alluvial tangents.

SOME LAGNIAPPE WITH THAT

LAGNIAPPE

From the Quechua *yapay* by way of the Spanish and with a French twist added in New Orleans, it means "a little extra." It's an old local custom. If you bought some red beans and some rice, the grocer might toss in a lagniappe onion. One morning I woke up in a New Orleans hotel room, stretched, went into the bathroom, looked in the mirror, and saw to my astonishment that I had a big, thick gout of dried blood in the middle of my forehead. I said to myself, I had better change my way of living. I could remember doing several things the night before, but not, for the life of me, being shot. It was Winston Churchill, I believe, who said that the most exhilarating experience in life is to be shot at and missed. But to be shot at and hit, and have no recollection? Especially if you're a writer. But then I turned on the light and looked closer, and of course I had not been shot. I had just slept on my complimentary mint.

CREOLE

This term originally meant "born here," in reference to a fresh start in the New World. As the generations rolled on, people who claimed descent from the early French families used it to mean "from way back." Then, because New Orleans culture is such a mélange, people began to assume it meant "mixed race," which caused light-skinned Creoles to deny that there was any such thing as a Creole of color. All along there were descendents of early black, brown, and beige natives of the city who duly considered themselves to be Creoles (says *Times-Picayune* columnist Lolis Elie, "A white guy told me he never heard of any black people called Creoles. I told him I never heard of any white people called Creoles"), and indeed in recent years anti-Eurocentric studies have controlled the discourse to the point that in both scholarly and popular circles Creole is most likely to connote old African-Louisianan blood. Or a culture so blended that there's no separating one ethnic strain from another. Categories melt in New Orleans.

Alligator sausage

"What does alligator taste like?" people would occasionally be heard to ask at the Tally Ho. "Like alligator," would be the answer, after a beat.

Beignet

A square doughnut with no hole. Which may seem contradictory, but then New Orleans is a laissez-faire city developed for French Catholics by a Scot named John Law whose architecture mostly reflects the Spanish occupation imposed by troops under Don Alexander O'Reilly.

Small coffee

Don't order the large, because the cup, tall but not so big around, is hard to dunk into.

Chuck Berry

In his autobiography he writes that New Orleans was "a place I'd longed to visit ever since hearing Muddy Waters's lyrics, 'Going down to Louisana, way down behind the sun.'" His first trip there was to perform, in 1955. After the thrill of "seeing my black name posted all over town in one of the cities they brought the slaves through," he found that his black skin made him inadmissible to strip joints. Whenever he tried to peer into one, in fact, the doorman "would draw the door closed as I strolled past, reopening it beyond my sight." So, after putting on a show that went over big ("Maybe someday your name will be in lights, saying 'Johnny B. Goode Tonight' "), he went back to Rampart Street, where the strip clubs were back then, and "employed a little strategy of my own. With the exception of when the door would close because a black male happened to pass in front . . . I enjoyed a half dozen full shows wearing a cowboy hat and gloves, standing in doorways and using my field glasses from across the street."

Mark Twain

He came here in February of 1857, at twenty-one, hoping to catch a ship to South America, where he would make his fortune from the importing of coca leaves. Fortunately for modern American literature, which might otherwise have kicked off with *Fear and Llamas at Lake Titicaca,* the coca thing didn't pan out, so young Sam Clemens signed on as a cub pilot on a riverboat instead. Back and forth up and down the Mississippi, in and out of New Orleans. To have some spending money for the nightlife there, he would guard piles of freight on the levee. "It was a desolate experience, watching there in the dark among those piles of freight; not a sound, not a living creature astir. But it was not a profitless one: I used to have inspirations as I sat there alone those nights. I used to imagine all sorts of situations and possibilities. . . . I can trace the effect of those nights through most of my books in one way and another." When the Civil War broke out, Clemens got off the boat in New Orleans and said good-bye to piloting. After a couple of weeks as a Confederate irregular, he headed out west. In 1881 he returned to the river to expand his recollections for *Life on the Mississippi,* several of whose chapters are about New Orleans.

W.C. HANDY

Struggling to make it as a musician, he was penniless in New Orleans. No place to lay his head at night but the levee. It was hard bedding, he recalled years later, and that is why his "St. Louis Blues" begins, "I hate to see that evening sun go down."

INGRID BERGMAN

The movie is *Saratoga Trunk,* from the novel by Edna Ferber. It was filmed on Hollywood sets (as were Elvis in *King Creole,* Mario Lanza in *The Toast of New Orleans,* which Pauline Kael called "sheer excruciation," and *Naughty Marietta,* in which Jeanette MacDonald and Nelson Eddy find in New Orleans, at last, the "ah, sweet mystery of life"), but most of the story takes place in New Orleans during Reconstruction.

Bergman is the fabulous, amoral, *brunette* adventuress Clio Dulaine, who returns from Paris to claim her Creole birthright. With her are her dwarf manservant Cupidon

and her ominous maidservant played by Flora Robson—
"the least likely mulatto," as Kael noted, "in the history of
cinema," with kohl-surrounded gimlet eyes. Gary Cooper
plays Clint Maroon, a gambler from Texas. (Cooper was
drawn to the project by the fully sufficient circumstance
that he and Bergman had started an affair on their previous
picture, *For Whom the Bell Tolls,* in which she played a pal-
pable but virtually mute blond Spanish revolutionary love-
bunny. The noted harmonica player Larry Adler saw
Saratoga Trunk and told Bergman she was miscast—she was
a wholesome Swedish girl. Though this hurt her feelings,
she had an affair with him.)

To be precise, it is off a plate atop the hat on Cupidon's head that Clio enjoys jambalaya, she and he both
standing, in the French Market. Bergman eats! Later it's
fresh peaches submerged in champagne, *in the daytime,*
after which she sleeps for two days.

A lawyer sent by her relatives tries to bribe her into
leaving town, but he can't concentrate. Halfway through
the business proposition in question, he blurts: "You're
beautiful!"

"Yes," she says, "isn't it lucky?"

Clint, impulsively, to Clio: "I love hearing your voice.
It goes over me like oil over a blister. Folks back home are
fine but they got kinda squeaky voices."

Clio, manipulatively, to Clint: "I love you like the pig
loves the mud." Clint, or maybe Gary, looks a bit taken
aback by this. But not so aback as Clio is taken when she

learns that Clint isn't rich. After making the most of her presence in New Orleans she moves on to Saratoga, New York, where just as her engagement to a boring man of wealth is about to be announced, Clint bursts into the party. In the course of a business matter he has been beaten half to death with a shovel, and he is *carrying the dwarf*—who may *be* dead—under his arm. Clint has made his fortune, two-fistedly, and of course he was the man for her anyway, and the dwarf comes to. It is a *great* bad movie, whose richness springs from New Orleans.

CREATIVES

Once, during some literary conference or another, the writer Molly Ivins, the artist Polly King, and I accompanied the former wife of David Bowie, who had a spicy memoir out, to a French Quarter apartment where "the widder Bowie," as Molly would call her afterward, was staying with a friend who painted startlingly lurid figure studies. All I remember of the conversation is that the widder Bowie's end of it was conducted at very nearly the top of her lungs, as if she were trying to be heard, or to hear herself, over a David Bowie concert; and that we all happened to agree at one point that we liked spring. I think it was spring. We all turned out to be pretty much on the same page there, causing our hostess to observe, "Well, we're all creatives." (Other creatives who had flings with New Orleans include Katherine Anne Porter, Malcolm Lowry, Sinclair Lewis, Nelson Algren, Erskine Caldwell,

Thornton Wilder, Pete Maravich, and Jorge Luis Borges, who subsequently wrote a story about a squeamish famished man who in trying to swallow his first oyster . . . no, I'm just making that up.)

Fats Domino

The man who found a generation's thrill on Blueberry Hill is long retired but still residing in his big pink-and-yellow-trimmed fifties ranch house in the Ninth Ward. He gives no interviews. Some years ago a famous local TV news guy, Phil Johnson, who was famous for his pretentious nightly editorial and the way he intoned "Good evening," resolved to get Fats for his show. He knocked on Fats's door. Fats opened it. "Hey, it's Phil Johnson!" said Fats. Phil Johnson beamed. Said he was there to interview Fats. "Hey, say 'Good evening' for me," said Fats. Phil Johnson didn't want to, but Fats said oh, come on. So Phil Johnson said it. "Come next door and say it to my neighbor," Fats said. Phil Johnson didn't want to, but he did. "Now my other neighbor," said Fats. Phil Johnson didn't want to, but he did. "Now one more neighbor, over here, they'd love it, it would mean so much to them," Fats said. So Phil Johnson did. Fats had him all up and down the street saying "Good evening" to everybody. Finally, Phil Johnson asked was Fats ready to do the interview now. "I don't do interviews," Fats said.

In *OffBeat* in 1997, the director of WWOZ (a wonderful roots-music radio station that is always on the verge of folding) spoke of being privileged to eat Fats Domino's cooking: "It was the first and only time I'll ever eat barbe-cued pickled pig lips. If Fats is cooking in his backyard, you got to eat it. They weren't as tough as you'd think. At least the grill burned off the hairs. Fats has a funny diet."

JEFFERSON DAVIS

In the Confederate Museum on Camp Street, with portico and tower in the style of Louisiana native H. H. Richard-son, the first truly American architect, is displayed a crown of thorns that Pope Pius IX made and sent to Davis when he was in prison after the war. A card next to it says: "Davis was deeply touched and he had a special need of cheer at this time, 'when,' as he said, 'the invention of malignants was taxed to the utmost to fabricate defamations to de-grade me in the estimation of mankind.' "

BOTH MARIE LAVEAUS

Mother and daughter, they are remembered as one: the Voodoo Queen, who led rites that may have involved naked dancing (and sometimes, it is said, respectable citizens), and who are said to have exerted political power over a considerable stretch of the nineteenth century. People still chalk X-marks on their tombs in St. Louis Cemeteries No. 1 and No. 2. Some fifteen percent of the city's population still practices voodoo, it is said, but the reason you are advised not to visit these graves alone is the percentage of the population that unquestionably practices mugging.

Gertrude Stein

She came in 1934 to lecture and to visit Sherwood Anderson. She wrote that she and Alice B. Toklas were shown "the social register of the bawdy houses and a charming little blue book with the simple advertisements of the ladies by themselves and we have eaten oysters a la Rockefeller and innumerable shrimps made in every way and all delicious and we are taken to visit the last of the Creoles in her original house unchanged for 100 years . . . all very lovely and lively."

Ramble One: Orientation

Mitch: I thought you were straight.
Blanche: What's straight? A road or a line can be
straight. But the human heart?

—A STREETCAR NAMED DESIRE

SINCE THE MISSISSIPPI FLOWS GENERALLY SOUTH FROM ITS origin in Minnesota to the Gulf of Mexico, you expect a town on the river to be on the east bank or the west. But at New Orleans the river flows eastwardly, sort of, so New Orleans is on the north bank, sort of. On the other side of the river is an area known, to be sure, as West Bank, but most of it lies either south or east of the river. On a map you can see: if the river were straight, New Orleans would be almost horizontal, right to left, east to west, between the river to the south and Lake Pontchartrain (as big as Rhode Island) to the north. But the river is crooked.

The best known parts of New Orleans form a sort of tipped-forward *S* along bends in the river, from Uptown and the Garden District through Downtown, the French Quarter, and on around eastward into Fauxborg Marigny and the Bywater. Within this *S,* Uptown is south (upriver) and Downtown north (downriver), because the river takes a northerly hitch. However, the part of the Quarter that is farthest downtown is referred to as the upper Quarter, though I have heard it called the lower.

So when I tell you that I am pretty damn sure that in 1998, during Hurricane Georges, I saw the river, at least the topmost layer of it, flowing backward (because the wind was blowing so hard southerly along that northerly hitch), you can see why I might not be absolutely sure.

It was late and I was by myself at the time, nobody else was around. And I was feeling let down, because although the wind was blowing hard, and half the population had been evacuated, and thousands who'd stayed had been herded into the Superdome for their safety, and my friend Greg Jaynes and I had taken refuge in the shuttered-up Burgundy Street home of my friend Curtis Wilkie, it was clear that this was not going to be the Big One: the full force of Georges was going to miss us.

We knew this from Nash Roberts. Nash Roberts is a veteran New Orleans TV weatherman who is low-tech, at least by way of presentation, and always right. Nash was broadcasting from his own house, it looked like, tracing the hurricane with a grease pencil on a sheet of Plexiglas

or a pad of paper, I forget which, while the other chan-
nels' meteorologists were using all manner of laser point-
ers and rear-projected electronic schematic representations
of the area. You couldn't tell what in the world Nash was
scribbling with the grease pencil, but as usual he was the
first to make the call, this one's going to miss us, and he
was on the money.

So I felt I could venture outside and take a look at the
river, and when I did, it was going backward. I'm pretty
damn sure.

Ordinarily, at any rate, when you face the river from
the French Quarter you'll see the river flowing from your
right to your left. As recently as the late sixties, early seventies, when Kermit Ruffins was a kid in New Orleans—
he's a fixture in the city now as a jazz musician—he'd
catch crabs from the river, to eat. "Get some string, tie a
chicken leg on it, and when that string get real tight, pull
in real slow—scoop 'em up and put 'em in the bucket.
End of the day we might have a hundred, hundred-fifty
crabs." You wouldn't want to eat anything out of the
river here now; it's filthy with silt and petrochemicals. But
it's a robust presence. John Barry, author of *Rising Tide,* a
terrific book about the horrific flood of 1927 (which the
New Orleans elite managed to divert onto poorer folks'
lands) says the river is "perfect," as opposed to the imperfect people who try to make it behave. It's a little like
the horse that the New Orleans "swamp blues" musician
Coco Robichaux told me about, which kept walking

into a post, over and over. "What are you doing trying to sell a blind horse?" somebody said. "He ain't blind," said the man who was trying to sell him. "He's just tough. He don't care."

The river is perfect because it doesn't care. It would just as soon drown New Orleans, or any other place, as not. But people, being imperfect, want to believe that it cares. People call it "Old Man River," "The Father of Waters." Big dirty thruster barreling into town.

And New Orleans, née *La Nouvelle Orleans,* is ready to take him on. Not "ready" in the sense that she has pulled herself together for their ultimate date yet (efforts are under way to figure out how to build a wall or something), but she wouldn't be herself if she were all squared away. Stephanie Dupuy, a native New Orleanian, once quoted Billy Wilder on Marilyn Monroe to relevant effect here. Stephanie and I were in Jennifer Flowers's club listening to her sing "Happy Birthday" in a breathy voice, and let it be said that she, who had a long affair with Bill Clinton, did not belabor the allusion by singing it explicitly to "Mr. President." Stephanie works out of the mayor's office, coordinating with people making movies in the city. She says that when movie people come to New Orleans, they say the same thing Meyer Lansky said when he discovered Batista's Cuba: "At last, a government I can work with." Stephanie knows Hollywood lore. She says that when people on the set of *Some Like It Hot* were complaining that Marilyn was always late, Wilder, the director, said this: "I have an aunt in Austria who is always on time. You want her to play the part?"

Orientation. You're in the French Quarter looking at the river. Now turn around and repeat this mnemonic: *D*ixie *C*ups, *R*ock 'n' *B*owl, *D*ucks *B*y *R*uthie. The Dixie Cups were a sweet and snappy New Orleans trio, two sisters and a cousin, who knocked the Beatles off the top of the charts with "Chapel of Love" and had another big hit with "Iko, Iko," the old Mardis Gras chant. (New Orleans has a long history of musical families, the Boswells, the Nevilles, the Marsalises, Harry Connick Jr. and Sr.—senior having retired as the city's district attorney to appear as "the singing DA.") Rock 'n' Bowl is an uptown bowling alley (Mid-City Lanes) that is also where you can dance till all hours to, say, the zydeco stylings of Boozoo Chavis. And Ruthie is perhaps the most famous French Quarter character, who used to rollerskate around the Quarter followed by a string of ducks. *D* is for Decatur, *C* for Chartres, *R* for Royal, *B* for Bourbon, *D* for Dauphine, *B* for Burgundy (pronounced with the accent on *gun*), *R* for Rampart, the long streets of the Quarter in order.

The order of the short streets that cross the long ones may be borne in mind as follows: "*C*'mon, *I*'ll *B*e *C*ool, *S*ugar, *T*ake *S*omething *O*ff—*S*omething *D*ainty, *S*ome *U*nderwear—*G*o, *B*aby, *E*verything!" Canal, Iberville, Bienville, Conti, St. Louis, Toulouse, St. Peter, Orleans, St. Ann, Dumaine, St. Philip, Ursulines, Governor Nichols, Barracks, Esplanade. To keep the sequence of the saint streets straight, remember, Louis, Peter, Ann, Philip: "*Let's Party And Party.*" These are my own mnemonics, which may not suit everyone, but you are welcome to share them.

We will walk beyond the Quarter, but this is the old city, the Vieux Carré, the central, original, the part of the city that is most . . . how shall I put it? The music critic Will Friedwald praises Connie Boswell's singing as follows: "Unlike [Mildred] Bailey's thin, delicate wisp, which, though charming, represented a coy middle-American attitude toward sex, Boswell's is a more directly sensual, genuinely vaginal instrument, something else [aside from the influence of Louis Armstrong] she picked up in New Orleans." It is said that the French founders of the city, when they couched its name in the feminine gender, as opposed to *Le Nouveau,* were making a bit of a joke: the Duke of Orleans, for whom it was named, was known to wear women's underwear. But if a city may be regarded as having a sex, surely Chicago for instance is male, New Orleans female. And the Quarter, for all the rectilinearity of its grid, is the most vaginal part of town.

LAGNIAPPE WITH ORIENTATION

Genifer Flowers

For a time early in the twenty-first century, she and her husband Finis D. (forgive me if I have the middle initial wrong) Shelnut operated a club in the Quarter where she sang. I had a chat with her between sets, a good-looking woman not at all stuck up. She sang pretty, too. "It Was Just One of Those Things," which she modified slightly for two patrons who said they were from Buffalo ("a trip to the moon on Buffalo wings"), and "You Make Me Feel Like a Natural Woman." Shelnut himself stood over in a corner listening. J.F. winked at him and said, "My husband went to the doctor, wasn't feeling good. The doctor said, 'You need to have sex five times a week.' My husband told me, and I said, 'Put me down for two of those.' " Finis (pronounced Fine-iss) produced an enigmatic smile. In the audience, dancing to the music, wearing a round red hat snugly attached to a brunette wig, was the lively octogenarian Verita Thompson, who had earlier presided over a club on the same site called Bogie and Me, in reference to her having been Humphrey Bogart's mistress, an association evolving from her service as custodian of his toupee: "She was his hairist," said Stephanie Dupuy, who introduced us as Verita boogied by. A man standing near us jumped. "I've just been groped by an eighty-year-old woman," he confided.

Rock 'n' Bowl

An event that was scheduled for that venue in 2002, according to Bunny Matthews in *OffBeat:*

> *Ernie K-Doe has never let a minor obstacle like death get in the way of his imperial career. His widow, Antoinette K-Doe, is producing an extravaganza on September*

*20. . . . At approximately 8:30 p.m., the wax statue
of K-Doe will be transported via the Mother-in-Law
Van from the Mother-in-Law Lounge to Mid-City
Lanes. . . . At the bowling alley, the statue will be
transferred to the K-Doemobile (a vehicle based on the
Popemobile) and escorted into the club, attended by the
Paradise Ladies (Antoinette and Uptown snowball stand
proprietress T-Eva) and the Cleopatra Ladies (a bevy of
dancers . . .). Inside Rock 'n' Bowl, music will be pro-
vided by the Blue-Eye Soul Band, Al "Carnival Time"
Johnson, Oliver "Who Shot the La La?" Morgan, Rico
Watts (impersonating Elvis Presley) . . . And, at some
point in the evening, Antoinette will don a wedding
gown à la Priscilla Presley and the wax rendition of
K-Doe will sing "White Boy/Black Boy" and "Children of the World." Don't ask me how.*

Hurricanes

A hurricane, as it approaches New Orleans or lurks off-
shore, becomes a character in the local media and in local
conversation (for instance Isidore, of 2002, seen as sulking,
lumbering, fickle), its arc and potential a matter of debate
and speculation, as if the storm were a candidate for public office. Very little dread seems to enter into the discus-
sion—for one thing, as the Louisiana novelist Jim Wilcox
observes, hurricanes are a great relief from the heat. However, he says, "There is nothing like the heat the day after
a hurricane."

Ramble Two: Wetness

Perspiration is healthy. If people didn't perspire, they'd die in ten minutes.

—Blanche DuBois

SURELY ONE REASON NEW ORLEANIANS TAKE THE threat of inundation so lightly is that the city is so moist as a rule. Most months, people walking outdoors gain a sheen, which in the summer never quite goes away. You look through an open doorway into a courtyard to see lush plants being watered so lavishly that a stream pours out into the street. Watch your head—more water sluices down, from the watering of balcony ferns.

It can rain so hard in New Orleans that you expect to see alligators bouncing off the pavement: a sudden event, foreshadowed as suddenly by dark clouds painted onto a perfectly sunny day, and thunderclaps ripping the firmament. Also dramatic in their way are the soft showers of the early evening, sometimes arriving spookily in full sunshine from no clouds at all, or thick white ones like real whipped cream, and people say, "The devil is beating his wife." The Quarter is fine to walk in during a summer rain, with the balconies overhead protecting the stroller except intermittently when he or she, or preferably they, choose to cross a street. The streets glisten with the wet, there's a passing cleanliness in the air, which afterward may be hotter than ever, the smell of wet pavement evaporating in wisps of steam. Tennessee Williams wrote of "the quality light could not be expected to have again after rain, the pigeons and drunkards coming together from under the same stone arches, to move again in the sun's faint mumble of benediction with faint surprise."

The mist can add a patina to the replica riverboats that take tourists on excursions up and down the river. They look about as much like wedding cakes ("without the responsibility," as Mark Twain put it) as the original ones did, and quite competent musicians play old favorites on them, so if there is enough mist over the river you might hope, as the *Natchez* or the *Creole Queen* approaches, to summon up the vision that Jack Teagarden beheld, one evening in 1917 or so, as he rambled the Quarter.

Teagarden would go on to become a great jazz trombonist, but at this point he was still listening for a breakthrough groove. He heard a trumpet in the distance, over by the river, and took off in that direction. "I couldn't see anything but an excursion boat gliding through the mist back to port," he would recall in later years. "Then the tune was more distinct. The boat was still far off. But in the bow I could see a Negro standing in the wind, holding a trumpet high and sending out the most brilliant notes I had ever heard. It was jazz; it was what I had been hoping to hear. . . . I don't even know if it was 'Tiger Rag' or 'Panama.' But it was Louis Armstrong descending from the sky like a god."

The waterfront is not what it was before the Civil War, when the Mississippi was the nation's main avenue of commerce, and hundreds of riverboats and barges would be arriving or standing by there at once. Nor is it the *noir* huddle of wharves where Elia Kazan in 1949 shot Richard Widmark and Paul Douglas pursuing unwitting plague carriers Jack Palance and Zero Mostel in Elia Kazan's *Panic in the Streets.*

Nor was there anything divine about the sounds I heard mingling along the river one September afternoon, in 2003: a calliope on the passing riverboat booming the tune to "Can't You Hear the Whistle Blowing," and the soft rumble of a train on the track that parallels the river there, and a tooot-tooot from the train, and a streetcar clattering along another track, and a crossing signal going ding-ding-ding, and a flock of uniformed schoolkids chattering, and a guy fwoopily blowing up, squeakily tying, and doggedly hawking balloon animals: "Presto! Instant giraffe!" Then the riverboat blew its piercing contralto steam whistle, and the temporarily drowned-out balloon guy swung around toward the riverboat and hollered "WAS THAT NECESSARY?"

No, it wasn't. But the whole thing wasn't Disney World either. It was a confluence of noises mostly tourist-driven but not virtual. And a spatter of rain came through the colorful scene like a sloppy brushstroke of mineral spirits. I proceeded on down the riverside Moonwalk, a wooden promenade, to the Aquarium at the foot of Canal. Some years ago I made a speech there, at a fund-raising dinner connected with the Aquarium's opening. The audience, if that was the word, listened to my leisurely buildup for about five seconds and then fell to talking freely among themselves, reducing me to background noise. I guess musicians get inured to that, but it's embarrassing when you're making a speech, as I persisted in doing for a full half hour to make sure of getting paid. I learned then that you can't mosey up on a New Orleans audience, especially one that has been talking and drinking for some time. They've got too many other sources of pleasure working. If you don't jump right in and paddle hard, you're jetsam.

Every time I visit the Aquarium, I learn something. Once in the penguin enclosure, the keeper was sitting on a rock with penguins gathered all around him, wagging their tails and flapping their wings. It looked like he was telling them a story, but in fact he was giving a little talk to a small audience of people. Aquarium penguins can't be allowed to reproduce much within their narrow circle, he said, because the gene pool will be too shallow (at that, as if on cue, two penguins dove into the water and swooped along together), so plastic eggs are substituted for some of the real ones. But some chicks are born, and the "moms and dads" take turns tending to them, with help from friends who eat a bit more than their fill and drop by to regurgitate a snack for the little ones. Penguins, he said, are very soft to pet. They are covered not in patent leather, as it might appear, but by lots of tiny feathers, eighty to ninety to the square inch, as opposed to eight or nine in flying birds. One penguin named Patience would nuzzle the keeper like a cat when he scratched her head, and sulk when he stopped. A couple of the other penguins had found that they could gain the attention of attendants by untying or pooping on their shoes. The penguins' diet is fish, but one of them was scared so badly by a big steelhead trout placed in the tank that he stayed out of the water for days. At another display, I was able to touch a limpet named Patrick. Once somebody showing me around the Aquarium mentioned that a biologist doing an autopsy on a shark reached inside and was bitten by a fetal shark.

Early developers had in mind a grand canal along Canal Street, but it didn't pan out. Still it's a fine broad thoroughfare, formerly lined by deluxe theaters and emporia, later spooky and semi-abandoned (and the Quarter a slum), now a semi-refurbished mélange. The old S.H. Kress and Co. dime store and the former D.H. Holmes department store are now the Ritz-Carlton and the Chateau Sonesta. On the banquette in front of the latter stands a statue of Ignatius J. Reilly, the hero of John Kennedy Toole's famous comic New Orleans novel, *A Confederacy of Dunces.* The statue is not a good likeness: not fat enough and too sane.

Also on Canal is the mammoth old four-façaded, sixteen-columned marble U.S. Customs House—*not* built on bales of cotton, as tour guides will tell you. It is built on cypress beams. The bales that were laid down along the beams serve to soak up water, so the beams still haven't rotted away. The whole city-block-covering building, however, has sunk three feet. A friend of mine, Virginia Dabbs, works there. If you try to bring drugs into this country through the port of New Orleans, she says, you'd better not catch the nose of certain customs agents. "If a cocker spaniel sits down next to you," she says, "you are toast."

You can buy booze on Canal at any time. There are stores that specialize in liquor and luggage and beads and strange artifacts. For instance, a stuffed armadillo wearing this outfit: a cowboy hat, a sheriff's badge, and two six-shooters. No price tag.

"How much for that?"

"Oh, that's about $169."

"But the tag on this one, not dressed up, says $325."

"Yeah, that one's got to be $285. They're not cheap. 'Cause you got to pay the taxidermist. And he charges an arm and a leg."

Imagine being drunk enough to be pricing armadillos, to take back home in your new extra suitcase, and trying to do that math?

Down the middle of Canal is a track for the nation's oldest streetcar line in continuous operation. We will take that uptown—catching it at the corner of Canal and St. Charles, which is the uptown continuation of Royal.

Note, near the streetcar stop, an old, now unfortunately gussied-up, oyster bar called the Pearl. What I like most about it are the nicely rendered representations of oysters inlaid in the banquette outside. It can't have been easy to capture the essence of open-face oyster on a flat, hard surface. Each oyster is different, as to its white and its gray areas—not stylized, like the oyster-shaped light fixtures (their bulbs are their pearls) overhead inside.

You hop onto the streetcar, which rattles uptown. Soggy-but-moving air has always come in through the windows, bearing smells of subtropical plants, but now, I am informed as I write this, the cars are being air-conditioned. That is a bad idea. Conditioned air could be anywhere. There is no air like the air of New Orleans.

On the way uptown we'll go through the Central Business District, a jumble of monolithic contemporary office buildings and art galleries of interest, and the Superdome, where the New Orleans Saints of the National Football League play out their doom year after year. And we'll pass Lee Circle.

Mist can have a great effect on what you see in New

Orleans. One night I walked up St. Charles to Lee Circle to have it out with Robert E. Lee, he of noble stoicism, drastically out of place in New Orleans. I had just finished writing a brief biography of Lee, and was ready to move on from him and the Civil War in general, but first I intended to ask him a New Orleans–related question. No, not what Steve McQueen asks Tuesday Weld, rhetorically, in *The Cincinnati Kid,* the movie about high-stakes poker set in New Orleans: "What good is honor if you're dead?" Lee would have stared me down on that one, to which even McQueen comes up with an honorable answer. But by the time honor becomes the issue, we've all got our armor buckled on. And aren't there a lot of less-than-honorable questions that anyone would rather ask of Tuesday Weld?

Here's what I wanted to ask Marse Robert: "Oh, why didn't you ramble? After all these years in New Orleans, haven't you learned that everybody owes it to himself, and to those around him, to ramble *some*?" I don't mean screw around, I mean loosen up. I associate Lee with my father, who was honorable, who was self-sacrificially community-minded, who rarely took a drink, who died when he was sixty, three years younger than I am now. My mother was already worrying about his heart when he was only forty-nine. I wish my father had *laisser le bontemps rouler* more often. With me, for instance. But he was a child of hard times.

When I got to Lee Circle, where Lee's statue was

erected in 1884 upon a sixty-foot Doric column, he, like my father, was gone.

There was the absurdly lofty pedestal. But no General Lee! Well, the living statues who pose on Decatur Street in the Quarter are not sticklers. They'll talk to you, if you keep at them, or they'll take a break for lunch in plain sight. You might see a couple of them, one gold all over and one stone-colored, sitting on the curb eating po-boy sandwiches and indulging in shop talk. Did Lee come down sometimes and hang out at that bar over there, telling war stories with musicians kicking back after their gigs?

"You know, Bob," says a member of the New Orleans–based band Better Than Ezra (sometimes I think New Orleans is the pun capital of America), "if I can call you Bob, New Orleans surrendered to the United States, with rancor but few shots fired, in 1862, and New Orleans, unlike Richmond, didn't get burned."

"Indeed. New Orleans is too damp to stay lit."

General laughter.

But no. The column is white, the statue dark gray. Up close, Lee emerged from the mist, planted facing north against the indifferent ancient foe. Over in the Quarter, in Jackson Square, rough-hewn Andy Jackson sits on a rearing horse, but Lee the capital-C Cavalier is condemned to balance forever on the small end of a marble beam. Back in 1963, when I was a reporter at the *Times-Picayune,* that newspaper's office was in the statue's line of sight, but now the last great Lee of the great American Lees was looking at anonymous new office buildings and a droning Interstate overpass, and to the southwest, over the preeminent self-denier's shoulder, shone a neon peacock, the emblem of NBC affiliate WBSU-TV. I didn't have the heart to pick a bone with him. Instead I went to the bar myself and hung out.

The Circle Bar, formerly Fleur de Lee. Behind the bar was an enigmatic little mural the management had discovered when a layer of paint or wallpaper was removed: two old guys in chairs, one of them Lee presumably but indistinct, his face blotted out except for the beard. William Burroughs used to huddle with junkies on Lee Circle. Now, the Circle Bar's proprietor told me, homeless people use the grass around Lee's pedestal as a bathroom. I flipped through a copy of *OffBeat,* the New Orleans music weekly, in which Art Neville was quoted as saying, "People try to put you in the pigeonhole. They got that statue of Lee Circle, and they want you to be like that: don't you ever change. We wasn't made for no bag." I went on out into the moist night and left Lee high and dry.

You are well advised to get off the streetcar and walk around in the Garden District—fine old houses, dating back to the days when cotton prosperity enabled the conflation of bounteous income and easy leaving. Bursting monstrously through the banquettes and jammed up against palm trees are the roots of old live oaks, whose limbs overhang the streets. From the limbs along St. Charles hang immemorial glass Mardi Gras beads.

I have seen this figure: that every year at Mardi Gras, from floats, to people begging for them, *fifty-eight billion* beads are thrown. A good place to watch Mardi Gras parades is St. Charles Avenue—not during the frenetic last weekend that is most people's idea of Mardi Gras: "They say if you like drinking and fighting and running naked, then that's your crowd," as a cabdriver told me. No, the week before the saturnalia is when you should catch parades along St. Charles, in crowds comprising a wide range of New Orleanians from the rich and poor neighborhoods that jumble together nearby.

There is a house on St. Charles that is built to look like a wedding cake. And there's a mansion called Columns, now a restaurant and hotel, where Louis Malle shot *Pretty Baby,* with Brooke Shields playing a girl born in a whorehouse and Susan Sarandon her mother. For $160 you can spend the night in the "Pretty Baby Suite," where as I recall Brooke's character lost her auctioned-off virginity.

And as you walk along St. Charles you may come upon the apparent shambles of an old horsedrawn sort-of-medicine-show cart, listing to the side, from which a man will sell you twelve pieces of "Roman Candy"—saltwater taffy—for five dollars.

I suggest you get off the streetcar at Audubon Park, where you can walk along a lagoon and over to a fine view of the river, and you can visit the zoo, whose orangutans are an inspiration for anyone with tight shoulders. Watch an orangutan *woop, woop, woop* its way along ropes to the top of a pole as high as Lee's column and sit there with those long arms folded, watching you. Maybe he'd rather be in a real rain forest, I don't know, but he looks more at home than Marse Robert.

The streetcar stops at Claiborne Avenue. A great deal of water is expelled, something to do with compressors, and the conductor comes along, *flack, flack, flack,* slapping the seats over so they face the other way for the trip back downtown. This time we could get off at Napoleon Avenue and walk toward the river, crossing Magazine Street, where the trendy shops are, to Tchoupitoulas (first syllable pronounced *Chop*), where we find Tipitina's, the storied music venue dedicated to the memory of Professor Longhair and his song "Tipitina" and still putting on good shows of everything from funk to Cajun till all hours. Also on Tchoupitoulas is the F&M Patio Bar, a cheerful neighborhood watering hole where some years ago the Queen of Comus stopped in after the ball, took off her shoes to dance, found the floor too dirty, and so became the first person to dance on the pool table. So many people have fallen off the pool table since then that a grating has been installed above it for dancers to grab on to.

Little early in the day for pool-table dancing, though. So let's go on back to the Quarter, where . . .

Where maybe we need a little break from the pictur-

esque? And something to relieve our head, because last
night those Sazerac cocktails at that great swanky art deco
bar in the Fairmont Hotel, formerly the Roosevelt, went
down so tasty and fast and, therefore, numerous? (They
used to contain absinthe; now, something called herbsaint.) Let's pop into the Walgreen's drugstore just down
Royal from Canal. Behind us in line at the cash register is
a jumpsuited, hardhatted man completely covered with
dust. He sees that we've purchased a generic headache
medicine, Wal-something, and he nods approval. "That
Wal- line is the way to go," he says. "I don't use that Slim-
fast, I use that Walfast—only thing is, it doesn't take me
up in the *middle,* know what I'm saying. I'm running up
and down thirty floors with the concrete all day—my
arms and legs lose weight, but the middle stay thick. Go to
make love to my wife and looking like Big Bird."

In New Orleans you can't get away from New Orleans, because people in New Orleans will talk to you. If a
woman you've never seen before addresses you as "baby,"
or "darlin'," it doesn't mean she's a hooker. She's just
being cordial. Her pronunciation of *darlin'* will very nearly
rhyme with the predominant local pronunciation of *Orleans.* It's sort of a cross between dahlin, dawlin, doilin,
d'ohlin, d'ahwlin . . . can't be spelled, it's an oral con-
struct. Similarly with *Quarter:* it comes closer to rhyming
with "porter" than with "garter," but it's more "Quo'-
tah," with an *o* sound that's semi-extended, as if you're
saying "oar," or "o'er" more like it, but not finishing off

the *r* sound. The essence is in that apostrophe somewhere. Something like that is going on in the word *oyster.*

Speaking of which, that concrete man looked awfully dry. Let's stop in at Felix's oyster bar, at Bourbon and Iberville, for a beer—sometimes even more effective than Wal-something—and lunch.

LAGNIAPPE WITH WETNESS

Audubon Aquarium
In 2002 at the Aquarium, a single bracket supporting a catwalk over an exhibit gave way, and ten people were dumped into a twenty-foot-deep tank filled with sharks. The people were in there swimming around terrified, some for as long as fifteen minutes, while the sharks circulated below their feet. No one was seriously injured.

The Cincinnati Kid
Edward R. Robinson slurps oysters, with relish. New Orleans movies tend to have some good eating in them.

Robert E. Lee
On a plaque outside the Old Absinthe House bar on Bourbon, you may see Lee's name, along with those of the Marquis de Lafayette, Jean Lafitte, Alexis Grand Duke of all the Russias, Oscar Wilde, Buffalo Bill Cody, Enrico Caruso, Sarah Bernhardt, John L. Sullivan (but not Jim

Corbett, who in 1892 at the Olympic Club on Royal Street took the heavyweight title from Sullivan in the first world championship bout fought with gloves), Babe Ruth, P. T. Barnum, and many other historical figures listed as having had a drink there. Not all together, but it's a nice thought. Lee did pass through New Orleans on his way to the Mexican War, but we may be sure that he eschewed anything like absinthe. Once I watched as Kappa Alpha fraternity brothers of Tulane University, in Confederate uniforms, and their dates in low-cut crinoline ball gowns, joked and posed for photographs at the base of his statue. He did love a cotillion.

WITH RANCOR

Clara Solomon, age sixteen, in her diary, 1862: "Endeavored to kill as few mosquitoes as possible. For two reasons, the first being that we should be polluted by being touched by 'Yankee blood,' and secondly each one increases the number and aids in biting and tormenting them. I wonder how they like them!"

MARDI GRAS

My favorite Mardi Gras participation has been walking with Curtis Wilkie's dog Binx—a dog with, as they say, a lot of "attaboy" in him—in Barkus, the parade of hundreds of dogs and dog people through the Quarter to Louis Armstrong Park, with a brass band right behind us.

Ramble Three: Oysters

I think oysters are more beautiful than any religion. . . .
They not only forgive our unkindness to them; they
justify it, they incite us to go on being perfectly horrid
to them. Once they arrive at the supper-table they seem
to enter thoroughly into the spirit of the thing. There's
nothing in Christianity or Buddhism that quite matches
the sympathetic unselfishness of an oyster.

—CLOVIS, CHARACTER IN A STORY BY SAKI

*I*T WAS AT FELIX'S THAT I FIRST ATE AN OYSTER RAW, that is to say live. A rite of passage. Felix's was a good place for it, because I don't like to be talked through things, and the shuckers in Felix's are not solicitous. As a rule New Orleanians in service occupations are by no means boundary-conscious. You'll hear a couple arguing at a restaurant table, the wife saying, "I need validation!"

and a passing waitress will say to the husband, "Yeah, *cher,* she needs validation." Rosemary James recalls entering a stylish restaurant and seeing one waiter slapping the other with a napkin as if challenging him to a duel, and the other pulling off a tablecloth to play him like a bull. "I realized," she said, "that everybody in the place was drunk." But the men who lay oysters bare at Felix's have perhaps been involved in so much opening up that they keep their own counsel. I loaded my first raw oyster with catsup, horseradish, hot sauce, and lemon juice, said a little prayer, and slurped it down.

It hit the spot. Now I eschew all seasoning but a spritz of lemon, and chew a few times for the savor before letting each little mollusk ease on down. Raw oysters give you a coolish inner lining collateral to the sheen that New Orleans humidity gives your skin. And I have seen too many people swallow oysters in Felix's in July without dying, to worry about the *r*'s in the month.

Across from Felix's Iberville entrance is another venerable oyster bar, the Acme. You are either an Acme person or a Felix's person. I am the latter. For one thing, in New Orleans oysters are pretty much oysters, because they come from farms in the brackish waters where the river meets the gulf. When the river has been low they have more flavor, because their habitat has been saltier, but they're seldom as flavorsome as Atlantic or Pacific ones. If you want splendid briny oysters, go to Apalachicola, Florida, where you can also get a local brand of hot sauce that proclaims itself "An Oyster's Best Friend." But there's no such thing as a bad oyster, unless they have *gone* bad. And there's often a line outside the Acme, whereas you can almost always walk into Felix's and lean against the place where the shuckers are shucking and call for a dozen and an Abita, the beer *du pays.*

At one point I resolved to capture the essence of New Orleans by tracing it through everything associated with the city, from the simplest form of life, the oyster, up the chain to the most complex: the prose style of William Faulkner. While writing his first novel, Faulkner lived for a time in a ground-floor room that is now part of Faulkner House Books, on Pirate's Alley, around the corner from St. Louis Cathedral. My friends Joe DeSalvo, who operates that excellent bookstore, and Rosemary James, founder of an annual literary festival celebrating New Orleans culture, now live above the store. At the end of the book, I figured, I could tie things up by quoting Faulkner on oysters. Maybe he had taken the point of view of an oyster, *whose life was all digestion suspended by ice now open to light not knowing it light yet knowing it the better for the flood of it once, just once, not knowing love nor lust nor even affection but just this fond violation of privacy by light, and knife, and now again dark, and digestion.*

If Faulkner ever wrote anything about oysters, I couldn't find it. Neither New Orleans nor my resolutions ever work out orderly. But in these times of culture-clash entanglements, when subjectivity vis-à-vis objectivity has become so vexed an issue, we might well dwell for a moment on the oyster. Why is Lewis Carroll's "Walrus and the Carpenter" such a lasting monument to cold-bloodedness?

> *"I weep for you," the Walrus said:*
> *"I deeply sympathize."*
> *With sobs and tears he sorted out*
> *Those of the largest size.*

Because who can honestly put himself in an oyster's place? A fish has a face, a snail a pace. An oyster, without its shell, is all morsel.

"Canst tell how an oyster makes his shell?" the Fool asks King Lear as he is being rendered homeless by his folly and his daughters. "No," says Lear. Can a grape coat itself in bark, a baby generate armor out of itself? An old man survive on his own?

Eating a raw oyster is like exchanging a soul kiss with the sea. But not much like it. We may think of Dickens's sanctimonious Mr. Pecksniff, and certain attempts to jog his memory:

> *"The name of those fabulous animals (pagan, I regret to say) who used to sing in the water, has quite escaped me."*
> *Mr. George Chuzzlewit suggested "Swans."*
> *"No," said Mr. Pecksniff. "Not swans. Very like swans, too. Thank you."*
> *The nephew . . . : "Oysters."*

"No," said Mr. Pecksniff, . . . "nor oysters. But by
no means unlike oysters; a very excellent idea; thank you,
my dear sir, very much. Wait. Sirens! Dear me! Sirens,
of course."

My memory is jogged by oysters. New Orleans
madeleines. In Felix's, especially, they make me think of
my friend Slick Lawson, photographer, who lived in
Nashville but hailed from Louisiana and loved New Orleans—maybe even more than I do, because he could stay
up longer. I'd stagger off to bed and he'd go find the bar
where the waiters went after work.

Over the years Slick and I went out into the Alabama
woods, to observe the Ku Klux Klan; and into the hills of
Hazard, Kentucky, to interview an opponent of strip mining (Slick was delighted when the man said, "You know
who owns this property here? Doris Day"); and to Paris
and the palace of Versailles to chronicle one of the many
political escapades of Edwin Edwards, then the roguish
governor of Louisiana, now in prison. In 1981, Slick and I
went to New Orleans for the orphans.

Parade magazine, for whom we had covered the Klan,
wanted us to do a heartwarming Christmas story on orphans. Sounded like a refreshing change from hanging
around with Klanfolk, who had made us feel like taking
a Lysol bath. My mother was an orphan. She had recently died. Slick and I were both fathers of children of
broken homes.

And we wanted, as always, to go to New Orleans. We figured we'd go to New Orleans and eat, drink, and— New Orleans had everything else, why not orphans?

We ate, we drank, and we discovered that orphans, strictly speaking, were an outmoded concept. The line of would-be adoptive parents was so long that almost any small American child left legally parentless would be snapped up. There were, however, plenty of troubled children who had been taken into custody by the state because their parents had abandoned, neglected, or abused them. These children weren't candidates for adoption because their wretched parents hadn't given up their rights to them. Nor had the kids given up their longing for the parents.

Some of these children could be placed temporarily with foster parents, but many of them had to become less troublesome first. They had to be weaned to some extent from their sense of what love was like. "These kids have never found handshakes and nods and smiles rewarding," said an administrator. "The only interaction that's gotten them attention has been negative and obnoxious."

So these kids were kept in group homes or other residences, where they could earn points for making eye contact, shaking hands firmly, and eschewing temper tantrums or at least cutting their tantrums back from hour-long to half-hour. If they accumulated enough points, they were told, they might be able to go back home.

"Adult attention is so important that kids will *take* violence," said a man who, with his wife, ran a group home.

"They'll *make* you mad at them." Because that's what it had taken to catch their parents' eyes. The man told of a boy who'd been "beaten by his mother. Badly. His body all . . . broken." When the boy cried, and the man's wife tried to comfort him, he'd say, "Nobody holds me when I hurt like my mama does."

"I'm a criminal," said one blond thirteen-year-old, with what seemed to be a mixture of bemusement and pride.

"No, you're not," said his teaching parent, a man whom the kids called "Zap" and whom we liked a lot. "You made some mistakes, but you're not a criminal."

"I stole a lawnmower," he said.

"A lawnmower?" I asked. "What did you want with a lawnmower?"

"His parents threw him out of the house," explained Zap. "He took the family lawnmower with him so he could support himself."

"I ain't staying here for no year," one boy told us. "I'm going *home*." He had recently complained, when served black-eyed peas and turnip greens, "We always get white people's food. I want some black people's food."

What did he call black people's food?

"Weenies," he said.

Another boy, "Ethan," practiced his "guest skills" by showing us around his group home. He showed everything, including the cabinet where they kept the salt. And the salt in the cabinet. Every time I turned to talk to another kid, Ethan showed me something else. And shook my hand. He had scars on his neck that looked like claw marks. He was earning points toward going back home.

"They come in here," an administrator told us, "with, oh, the mark of a barbecue grill on their back. Or . . . there is so much sexual abuse today." Some kids would go home and get beaten some more and have to come back. "And they still defend their parents to the death. If the other kids say, 'Your mama is mean,' they get mad. They say their parents are the best thing in the world."

Slick and I should have known that New Orleans was not the place to go for unalloyed heartwarming. We did find poignant loyalty. I didn't hear anybody say, "He ain't heavy, Father, he's my brother," but we met one nine-year-old who had been going from foster home to "residential treatment agency" to foster home since he was three, when authorities discovered that he was being left at home all day with a loaded revolver to guard his infant brother. And we met a ten-year-old whose twelve-year-old sister was in a different residence. Christmas was coming up. The administrator who introduced us told him he could list his first, second, and third choices from the Sears catalog.

"A tape recorder," he said, "and if I can't get that, a typewriter."

The administrator looked surprised. "You want a typewriter?" he said.

"No."

"But you said . . ."

"For my sister."

"What's your third choice?"

"A typewriter for my sister."

"That was your second choice. What's your third?"

"*A typewriter for my sister!*" he said.

Our problem, from a professional standpoint, was this: we couldn't report these children's real names, or tell their full stories, or take their pictures, because their parents might sue for invasion of privacy. The damn Klanspeople had welcomed publicity, but these kids might as well have been in a witness protection program.

Everywhere we went, the kids wanted to pose. Well, there was one girl who, with two kittens in her arms, declared, "You aren't going to take a picture of *me*. Like that man did in the paper once."

"Well," said Slick, "but if I *did,* where would you like to be photographed?"

"Standing over there on top of the monkey bars," she said.

She would have been perfect for the cover shot *Parade* wanted, but we couldn't shoot her. A boy came running up holding a flaxen-haired three-year-old, whom we will call "Greg." "I think Greg likes you," he said. "He keeps doing things and looking at you and saying, 'Daddy, watch!' "

Greg ran over toward the swings. An administrator said

Greg had been found, in a dirty diaper, with his sister, wrapped in a man's coat, and with his mother, who was eager to get rid of them because their father had ditched them all. Greg sat in the swing and said, "Daddy, watch," and did a somersault out of it. I said, "That's good, Greg," and his eyes lit up.

But no pictures. Then we heard of a small fundamentalist Christian institution on the outskirts of New Orleans that might be persuaded to let us get some touching shots.

We went there. Our mouths watered at all the cute kids we saw running around. We found the spiritual head of this institution reposing in a trailer home on the grounds. We were prepared to plead with him for pictures.

He was old, pale, and shapeless, a blob floating in the carapace of a Barcalounger. He breathed with a faint wheeze. He had had several bypass operations, he said, and was living only for his charges. Nestling nervously in the middle of him was an aged Chihuahua. We explained our mission, at length, as founder and dog eyed us narrowly.

Then we waited.

"On one condition," said the founder at last. A shudder went through the Chihuahua.

We waited.

He asked for a pen. I gave him one. He asked for paper. I tore him a scrap from my notebook. He wrote out a few words, slowly, deliberately, and handed the paper over. I believe he kept the pen.

His handwriting was spidery. His condition was "That it glorify Christ."

I looked at the message, Slick looked at it, and the man looked at us.

The Chihuahua sneezed, as if in disgust. A Chihuahua can tell who's from Satan.

In fact we behaved as Christians in that crucial moment. There was no one else around. We could with impunity have taken that dog and smothered the founder with it, and his consequent heart failure would not have surprised or stricken a living soul.

We did not do that. We let him live. He waved us away. No pictures. And no pictures, no story.

Slick and I went to Felix's. We kept up with the shucker through a couple of dozen, but after a while Slick wasn't eating so much as staring at the little pink bodies lying there exposed to the light. He started telling me about something that had happened when, as a teenager in Monroe, Louisiana, he was working as a lifeguard at an overcrowded pool. On his watch, a kid drowned. Nobody saw him go under. By the time anybody called for help, he was dead. Slick was full of remorse, especially when he heard that the child's parents wanted to have a talk with him. When they arrived, they just sat there looking at him. He expressed his deep regret, explained the situation as best he could, and got no response.

"I was about to cry, I felt so bad," he said.

Hard to imagine Slick in tears. He went on.

"The parents just stared. They looked nervous. I said, 'Is there anything you want to ask me?' Finally, the mother spoke up. She said, 'Can we have his frog feet?' "

Not a story *Parade*'s readers would want for Christmas. We had already run up quite an expense account. "What are we going to tell *Parade*?" I wondered aloud.

Slick stared at the oysters lying in their shells. It was early evening, magic time in terms of light, which was coming in through the big window there, lending a rosy glow. Slick picked up the battered Leica that stuck with him through thick and thin.

"How about: '*Orphans?* We thought you said *oysters.*"

MANY YEARS LATER, I'm in New Orleans alone, at Felix's, having a dozen and working the *New York Times* crossword. And the shucker is condescending to talk to me. He can evidently shuck and jive at the same time. He is telling me that the other night a man ate forty-eight dozen oysters at a sitting. Not here, but at a seafood place out by the lake. "I don't know if he even leaves the shells," he says. "Lives in Hammond, Loozanna. I wish I owned a grocery in Hammond."

"Fat?" I inquire.

"Yes. But not *extree-ordinarily* fat. About my heighth, with your stomach."

And in comes Becca. And her husband. I know who they are because he says, "Aw, Becca," and she looks at me, jerks her thumb over at him, and says, "My husband Kyle."

It's late fall, crispy for New Orleans, and she's wearing a sweater. Striped, horizontally, which on a flat surface would be straight across but on her the effect is topographical. And there's a twinkle in her eye—well, more of a glint, probably, but you can see seeing it as a twinkle in just the right light. "Shuck us a dozen," she tells the shucker, and with a look over at hubby, "Let's hope one of 'em works."

If I had not seen *Double Indemnity* enough times to be all too familiar with how these things turn out . . . Because she is over close to me now saying, "I work that puzzle every damn day of this world."

One look at Becca and I'm into a noir-narration frame of mind, thinking to myself, You know, a man has always got to be promoting getting some; and a woman always got to be promoting getting something out of giving some up; but a woman who is giving you some to get back at her husband can just enjoy it and let you just enjoy it because her ulterior motive is covered. Problem would be when she gets her message through to the husband, gets tired of that, and starts figuring out how you, too, are letting her down. I'd say Becca's daddy had money till she got halfway through high school and he lost it all: A daddy's girl whose daddy folded.

And now this husband, Kyle. A weedy sort. He nods

distantly, looking like he hopes it won't come across as miserably. "And two Ketels on the rocks," she says, and he says, "Aw, Becca," again. They're both fairly sloshed, but he's fading and she is on the rise.

" 'A little hard to find'? How many letters?" she says. She's up against my shoulder looking at the puzzle. Kyle's leaning against the counter, putting horseradish on the first oyster the shucker has presented them with. Without moving away from me or looking away from the puzzle, she reaches over, takes the oyster from in front of Kyle, puts it to her lips, gives me a little half-look, and slurps it down.

I say, "Eight."

She says, "A good man."

"But where's the 'little' in that?"

A woman just in it for the giggles would have made a coy face and said "I'm not touching that one." Becca gives me another half-look and grabs my pen and starts writing "A GOOD MAN" in.

That doesn't appeal to me at all, on one level. On another, it brings her up against me even closer.

She smells like her corsage—they're in town for the weekend, she says, for a football game—and her lipstick, maybe, which is certainly red enough to be aromatic, especially now that it's set off by a fleck of horseradish.

"No," I say, " 'A GOOD MAN' can't be right—see, fourteen down, 'Greek love,' would be AGAPE, and—"

She looks at me with both eyes, and rolls them. "Ooh, I don't think so, hon," she says. "Let's just jam it in there.

We'll make it fit." She writes AGAPE in so that the *E* is on top of the *N*.

That fleck of horseradish is still there on her lip. I could flick it off for her. Or I could point to the same spot on my own lip so she could get it off herself. I refrain from doing either.

Now she has one of my oysters. "Slurps" is too blatant. She takes it in juicily. Now she's filling things in one after another, free association and spontaneity being the key more than strict interpretation or even in some cases the right number of letters. I am more tolerant of this than I would be in other circumstances.

"You know we could do this all evening," she says, and in spite of my reserve I'm beginning to have the same thought. At this time I am unattached, and I am not thinking with as much edge as I was back there in that noir-narration frame of mind. But there's Kyle. She turns to him and says, "Me and this man could keep on doing this till another puzzle comes out." She takes the last of their dozen. "Kyle doesn't do the puzzle," she says. "Kyle could eat ever' got-damn oyster in New Orleans and he still couldn't do the puzzle. Let's go, Kyle, put some money down." He does, and my weight sags just a bit farther than I'd prefer in the direction of her abruptly withdrawn shoulder.

Becca and Kyle turn to go, her arm in his; but she looks back long enough to lick the fleck of horseradish off, finally, and to say, by way of farewell: "They like it when you dog 'em out."

I look at my puzzle, which is a mess.

"Say, 'They'?" says the shucker.

SLICK PULLED THE orphan story out of the fire. He had a wide circle of friends in, for instance, the ballooning and motocross and country-music communities, and one of them put him onto some photographable orphans. The cover picture, under the billing, "When Love Is the Best Gift of All—MERRY CHRISTMAS, AMERICA," was of a little blond girl who had been an orphan before adoption. But when Slick told the story of the orphan story he tended to leave people believing that we had shifted topics on *Parade* and pulled it off: *Oysters.* He pronounced it *oischers,* to rhyme with *moistures,* as do many people who savor those mollusks' juices. They say a mayor of New Orleans named DeMaestri hosted President Franklin Delano Roosevelt at dinner once and didn't say a word until the end of the evening, when he said, "How'd you like them ersters?" This is one of several indigenous pronunciations.

Some twenty years later Slick died, directly from drink. He was the second New Orleans rambling companion of mine who knew that drinking would kill him, who narrowly escaped dying once already from it, but went back to it anyway. One of the things Slick often said was, "I wouldn't want to live like that," in a not entirely facetious though mock-pious tone, pronouncing "live" sort of like "leeyuv." Say we passed a man in the street who was carrying a cat in a cage labeled "Tom Doodle" in fancy script, and the cat was emitting a cranky-sounding moan and the man was talking back to it in a whiny, put-upon voice. Slick would say, "I wouldn't want to leeyuv like that." When liquor began to get the better of him, he was in and out of rehab programs. "I'm drinking myself to death," he told me once, in tears. Slick, in tears! I told him drinking wasn't as much fun as it used to be, which was true. He agreed. A pleasure-principle grounds for abstention. But in the long run he couldn't live like that.

LAGNIAPPE WITH OYSTERS

SLICK'S LOVE OF NEW ORLEANS

One of his friends in town was the scion of an old family who fell in love with a stripper. The family was appalled, but the scion assured them that she was quite bright and cultured. Meet her and you'll see, he said.

So some of them came to the club where she worked, and sat talking to her, and sure enough she was quite the lady and well educated. They liked her. You couldn't not like her. Then she stood up and said, "Excuse me for a minute, y'all, I've got to go show 'em my monkey."

CHIHUAHUAS

On Decatur Street, across from the French Market, there's a wee nook called Chi-wa-wa Ga-ga, "A small store for dinky dogs." In the window in Christmas shopping season are many gift ideas, including a red-and-green sweater that says "I Don't Fa la la for Nobody," a pullover suit that would make a miniature dog look bulging with muscles, and nightlights for dogs.

Outside, a very large woman is holding in one arm a dog so diminutive and quivery that you can hardly make him out. She is saying to a heavy, beat-down-looking man, "Look, Rob, little crowns! It's a little dog store!" Halfway through the door, she sees Rob trying to continue down Decatur. She reaches back and grabs him.

I follow them inside, where many people are squeezing and milling about. At least seven of them have brought their tiny dogs, not all of whom are Chihuahuas. "Some kind of shelty and shih tzu, we don't know. Do we, Precious?" says one owner. One little dog, shivering on the glass counter, is modeling a tiara.

"She don't preshate it," says the man of the couple.

"Yes she does, she preshates it, don't you Weejee?" says the woman.

"She's already got one tiara. You going to get her another tiara she's not going to wear?"

Another little dog is brought to the counter, to try on a sweater. "It's too big for him, look, he's trying to get out of it. You have a changing room? He don't like to get naked."

Among the small dog toys for sale is a chewy-looking monkey labeled "Shake Me!" A shopper tells me, "Ohhh, my dogs back home have one of those, they love it so much." She shakes the monkey and nothing happens. "I can't get it to do," she says. "My dogs get it to do all the time. You try." I shake it for her, it emits a vaguely simian squeal, and she says, "There. That's what I hear all day long."

The *resident* Chihuahua sits next to the counter in a tiny stuffed armchair, yapping at everybody who tries to pet him.

"That your chair?" asks a woman trying to win him over.

"You're mighty god damn right it's my chair," says the Chihuahua.

BALLOONING

So far as I know, the full history of ballooning in New Orleans has never been told, but in 1858 two local enthusiasts, named Morat and Smith, raced from Congo Square to the corner of Camp and Felicity riding not in the standard gondolas, but on the backs of two live, eleven-foot alligators. And in a local paper in 1905 a man named Buddy Bottley (or Bartley), "the colored aeronaut," advertised "astonishing, perplexing, fascinating" balloon ascents. If Buddy brought along his brother Dude on these rides, to provide cultural commentary, they must have been fascinating indeed, judging by "old Mr. Dude Bottley's" recollections of early musical days in New Orleans, which appear in *Buddy Bolden and the Last Days of Storyville,* by Danny Barker. Bottley recalls hearing Bolden, in venues where the funk was like "burnt onions and train smoke," perform "such nice love songs," like "Your Mammy Don't Wear No Drawers, She Wears Six-Bit Overalls," "Don't Send Me No Roses 'Cause Shoes Is What I Need," and "Stick It Where You Stuck It Last Night." Bottley also speaks of a Lorenzo Staulz, who would sing Civil War songs "about how General Grant made Jeff Davis kiss and kiss his behind and how General Sherman burnt up Georgia riding on Robert E. Lee's back." Staulz "had a cleaning and pressing business. If you took your clothes to his place to have them cleaned, if he looked nice in your suit and it fitted him, he wore it. So, people naturally thought he had a hundred suits."

Ramble Four: Color

> *The various grades of the coloured people are designated by the French as follows . . . : Sacatra, [a cross between] griffe and negress; Griffe, negro and mulatto; Marabon, mulatto and griffe; Mulatto, white and negro; Quarteron, white and mulatto; Metif, white and quarteron; Meamelouc, white and metif; Quarteron, white and meamelouc; Sang-mele, white and quarteron. And all these, with the sub-varieties of them, French, Spanish, English, and Indian, and the sub-sub-varieties, such as Anglo-Indian-mulatto, I believe experts pretend to be able to distinguish. Whether distinguishable or not, it is certain they all exist in New Orleans.*
>
> —FREDERICK LAW OLMSTED, 1861

O N ESPECIALLY MISTY DAYS IN NEW ORLEANS, background colors emerge as if bleeding into the atmosphere: you catch sight of a beige-faced woman in a blue slicker carrying a manila envelope past a mint-green housefront, and it's as though you're seeing the color manila for the first time. In the Quarter and the Marigny and the Bywater, you see houses painted blue and green and white, orange and white and green, pink and beige, lavender and white and purple, ocher and powder blue, pink with red-and-white trim, aqua with cream trim and deep purple shutters.

New Orleans has historically been unconventional and recombinant also in regard to color of skin. The city from its founding in 1718 was a melange of voluntary European colonists, African and Indian slaves, and European deportees and indentured servants; there was much commonly accepted mixing of blood. Slaves escaped into the surrounding swamps and established "maroon" communities that traded with citizens of the town. And within a few decades there was a growing number of "free persons of color." Many of these were immigrants or refugees from Haiti (then Saint-Domingue), others former slaves who bought their freedom, or had it bought for them by relatives, in the late eighteenth century.

However, for most black Americans before Emancipation—for instance, for Jim in *Huckleberry Finn*—New Orleans was a threat: if they didn't toe the line, they could be sold "down the river" to the New Orleans market, which meant back-breaking labor and separation from loved ones in the deep South.

On a wall on the corner of Chartres and St. Louis,

there's a plaque with a bas-relief of three gents (one taller and more rawboned) looking at some papers around a table. The plaque commemorates "Original Pierre Maspero's Slave Exchange, est. 1788. Within this historic structure slaves were sold and Andrew Jackson met with the Lafitte Brothers and planned the defense for the historic and epic battle in which the British surrendered to American troops commanded by General Jackson. American independence was finalized and General Jackson went on to become the seventh President of the United States of America." The plaque doesn't linger even long enough for a comma after "slaves were sold." What the plaque might say is "slaves were sold to the highest bidder after being made to run, dance, leap, tumble, and twist to show they had no stiff joints, and after being fattened up over by the river in holding pens and washed in greasy water to make their skin shine." Until long after the finalization of American independence.

Slaves were sold at several locations in New Orleans. At the corner of Royal and St. Louis is the splendid, expensive Omni Royal Orleans hotel, on whose site once stood the even more opulent St. Louis Hotel, in whose rotunda slaves were auctioned off. An 1842 engraving of one such sale shows white men in big hats and white women in big dresses milling around as an auctioneer waves his gavel and points to a black woman naked above the waist. Also in the picture are two small black children not wearing anything and a black man with a wrap around his loins. In the foreground are casks and bales also up for auction. Louisiana law prohibited the sale of small children separate from the mother, but if they came from other states there were no restrictions. When the novelist John Galsworthy visited New Orleans in 1912, the St. Louis Hotel was in ruins. As he poked through them, he was startled nearly out of his skin by the sudden appearance of an abandoned, injured horse stumbling through the marble rubble.

As a young man, in 1828 and 1831, Abraham Lincoln twice worked his way on flatboats down the Ohio and the Mississippi to New Orleans. These exposures to what was then the nation's most cosmopolitan metropolis are assumed by biographers to have given Lincoln his first sense of the great world, and also his first sense of the magnitude and inhumanity of slavery. He'd seen some slaves in Illinois, but never anything like those auctions. According to a friend who accompanied Lincoln on his second trip, the sight of a girl being sold made him vow to do something about slavery when he got a chance.

New Orleans seceded along with the rest of Louisiana at the onset of the Civil War, but by April of 1862, Union troops had reclaimed the city. The Emancipation Proclamation, in 1863, abolished slavery only in those parts of the nation that were "in rebellion." According to *Soul by Soul,* Walter Johnson's authoritative history of the New Orleans slave market, "All signboards advertising slaves for sale in Union-held New Orleans were taken down on

January 1, 1864." So the slave trade continued for over a year in New Orleans after it came under the control of the Great Emancipator.

In 1873, when P. B. S. Pinchback, an African-American, was the Reconstruction governor of Louisiana, Edgar Degas had a long visit with relatives in New Orleans. He wrote back to Paris ecstatically of "the pretty pure-blooded women and the pretty quadroons and the strapping black women! . . . There are some real treasures as regards drawing and color in these forests of ebony. I shall be very surprised to live among white people only in Paris. And then I love silhouettes so much and these silhouettes walk." But the New Orleans light was too bright for his supersensitive eyes. He painted indoor scenes in which only a few glimpses of black folk appear. His mother's first cousin, a free New Orleanian of color named Norbert Rillieux, transformed the sugar industry and the sugar market by inventing a process for the efficient evaporation of murky cane juice into fine white grains. Sugar suddenly became so cheap to produce that just about any table could afford it, at least any white table, as long as there was plenty of cheap black labor. Reconstruction lasted longer in New Orleans than anywhere else, but local whites reassumed supremacist control after bloody riots instigated by a white citizens' militia, the White League.

Before things tightened up in the years leading to the Civil War, however, slaves had more freedom in New Orleans than elsewhere. They were allowed, notably, to assemble on Saturday nights to play drums, chant, and dance. The basic beat was known as Bamboula. The music that grew out of those get-togethers, absorbing Arabic, Italian, Catholic, and pop-American influences as it evolved, was jazz. Hip Northeasterners may sniff at "Dixieland" jazz, but bebop and Brubeck are inconceivable without the foundation laid by the tortuous, exuberant fusion that imploded in early New Orleans and expanded from there.

The gathering place for Bamboula was known as Congo Square, part of what is now known as Louis Armstrong Park. The New Orleans airport also is named for Armstrong now. Armstrong grew up in the streets of the city, marching with brass bands and soaking up street vendors' calls and ferociously rhythmic emanations from the clubs where musicians competed to establish themselves as the best in town. "They didn't have all the noise that you have today, like automobiles and trucks," remembered Danny Barker, who went back to the early days of New Orleans music, "and you could hear that beautiful calliope on the river," and other eruptions of music all around. "It was like the Aurora Borealis. The sounds of men playing would be so clear, but we wouldn't be sure where they were coming from. So we'd start running—'It's this way!' 'It's this way!'—And, sometimes, after running for a while, you'd find that you were nowhere near that music. But the music could come on you any time like that. The city was full of the sounds of music."

Armstrong got serious about his playing after he was

arrested for juvenile disorder in the streets (firing off a pistol for fun) and sent to a Catholic orphanage, where he studied cornet and played in the school's band. Later he was nurtured, to his lasting gratitude, by a Jewish family in town. As soon as he could, he headed upriver to Chicago and New York. But he kept on signing his letters "red beans and ricely yours." Traditionally, New Orleans music has been about "playing for the people," not just for the improviser and a coterie. The prime of Louis Armstrong was a time when the most serious music in America was also its sweatiest, downest, most joyous and engaging.

Today authorities recurrently try to clear the "betcha I can tellya whereya got them shoes" boys off the streets. My friend Lolis Elie, whose father was an eminent civil rights activist, argues that this is for the kids' own good: "They're not trying to be better, like Armstrong did. It's not about learning anything, trying to outdance each other. It's being out of school picking up change." But I hated seeing a fat white man running out of the Tropical Isle bar on Bourbon to shoo away five kids—two drums, a trumpet, a tuba, and a trombone—who were raising money to go on the George Washington Carver High School band trip, because tourists were listening to them instead of coming into his cheesy club. And there can be no excusing the city's efforts (futile as they seem to be) to discourage the cheerful a cappella doo-wop men who will serenade you and your sweetheart on the street for a dollar or so.

There are plenty of clubs in town where you can hear

good music for not much money, for instance Donna's and the Funky Butt on Rampart, Snug Harbor in the Marigny, and Vaughn's in the Bywater, where Kermit Ruffins holds forth on Thursday nights. Young musicians in New Orleans keep coming up with new variations on old traditions, for instance the Bounce, merging the Bamboula beat and brass-band blare and boop with rap: oompah-hop. In the window of a club called Mama's Blues on Rampart, I saw this clipping pasted: "Praline Soul. As one of today's most progressive young artists, 'MYSELF' comes from the heart and speaks to your soul. While (X)ploring hip hop and (re)defining poetry in motion, he pushes the new-soul movement to limitless boundaries . . . , embraces the conscious sounds of yesterday at the same time moving forward at the lightspeed of rhyme. . . . Hypnotic riddims with a rootsy vibe. . . . 'MYSELF' is formerly known as Goldielox."

You can further your education in New Orleans roots music by listening to WWOZ and shopping at great record stores like Louisiana Music Factory on Decatur or the Magic Bus on Conti. Or you can walk down Bourbon past various touristy clubs and take in an overlapping, well-rendered continuum of "St. Louis Blues," "Dock of the Bay," "Highway to Hell," "Don't Mess With My Toot-Toot," "Killing Me Softly With His Song," "Has Anybody Seen My Gal," "Shake Your Booty," and a guy with a great bass voice hollering "Jell-O Shots." You can hear all that for free, but it's only fair to stop into these venues long enough to drop a few dollars. And don't forget to tip the band. There is such a surfeit of musicians in town that they may well be getting paid only ten or twelve dollars apiece for the night.

The current mayor of New Orleans is black, as was his predecessor, but the city is hardly a model of racial harmony. You're not advised to venture too far afoot at night, because there is no shortage of poverty, drugs, and deadly weapons in town, and tourists are easy prey. I've always counted on being too large, irritable-looking, and ill-dressed to be a high-percentage target, but one afternoon just before twilight I was walking along Esplanade past gracious housefronts when two sizable African-American youths nodded as they passed me coming the other way. I nodded back. Then from behind I heard one of them cry, "Hey, buddy! Hey, buddy!" A young, professional-looking black man jogging ahead of me took one look back and sped up away from there. I looked back. "Remember me?" said the youth who'd called out. "You know, over by Rita's place?" He came toward me, holding out his hand to shake. There was nobody else around. I didn't know any Rita, so I said, "You don't know me," and picked up my pace in a hurry.

When you're going anywhere in New Orleans that you've never been before, it's a good idea to phone for a United cab. It's not a touristy thing to do. Old ladies living alone in the Garden District call United to bring them vodka and cigarettes in the middle of the night. There are other taxi companies, but everybody I know in town says, "Don't get excited, call United." A cab will be there in a jiffy, to take you anywhere you want to go, though one driver told me he hated to venture into the area of Tulane University because he had been stiffed too many times by college students. The drivers tend to be locals. One told me he'd moved to Atlanta, "but I had to move back. Atlanta made me feel like a little child. I don't even drink, but I don't want anybody telling me I have to stop, and go home, at a certain time."

LAGNIAPPE WITH COLOR

ROYAL STREET
Once on Royal Street I came upon a crowd that was cheering and groaning strangely. A man was lying in the middle of the street, agonizingly working his way out of a straitjacket. He dislocated one shoulder, then the other. In the end he was beet-red and scraped up, but free to pass a can around for change.

THE ROYAL ORLEANS
Its Rib Room provides excellent expensive food—New Orleans cooks can do steak as inventively as oysters—and also an opportunity to eavesdrop on high-rolling businessmen, like the two I overheard indulging in petrochemical nostalgia: "Before EPA, hell, we'd dump shit, when it

came out, the hairs on your arms would sizzle—but you could do that back then."

"That's right. I was in Thailand coming upriver to where we were building a refinery, and all of a sudden, what'd we hit? We ran into this village's whole fishing industry. It's a trotline all across the river, hand-woven out of bark, must've taken years, beautiful thing. I said, 'I'm not going to cut that,' but of course, had to. We wound up destroying that village. Houses, trees . . ."

"It was a different world back then."

Ramble Five: Food

Oyster Inspiration of the Day: The chef's creation,
from the classics to the unique.

—THE MENU OF THE 201 RESTAURANT
ON DECATUR

THE THING I HAVE WRITTEN THAT PEOPLE SEEM TO remember most is a song to oysters:

> *I like to eat an uncooked oyster.*
> *Nothing's slicker, nothing's moister*
> *Nothing's easier on your gorge,*
> *Or when the time comes, to dischorge.*
> *But not to let it too long rest*
> *Within your mouth is always best.*
> *For if your mind dwells on an oyster,*
> *Nothing's slicker, nothing's moister.*

ROY BLOUNT JR.

> *I prefer my oyster fried.*
> *Then I'm sure my oyster's died.*

In those last two lines, I lied. An oyster no more *needs* cooking than a sonnet by Shakespeare needs recitation. But when H. L. Mencken wrote that "No civilized man, save perhaps in mere bravado, would voluntarily eat a fried oyster," he revealed that he had never had a fried-oyster sandwich on homemade bread in Casamento's, the venerable shiny-tiled seafood house in Uptown New Orleans. It is a crime without question to fry an oyster so callously that the animal's integrity is lost, but an oyster that is still juicy and plump within a light layer of deftly seasoned crunch—in fact, *more* juicy and plump for the frying—is a sonnet set respectfully to a tune anyone can sing.

New Orleans is the best town for eating in America, if not in the world. There is high cuisine aplenty. I sing now of the spinach gnocchi and sauteed drum at Gautreau's, uptown. Of the tomato and ginger soup at Herbsaint, in the Central Business District. Of the chicken Rosmarino at Irene's, in the Quarter: chicken cooked in garlic and rosemary, which is such a signature dish that it is what Irene's smells like for the length of the block. Of the pistachio-crusted tenderloin of rabbit or the grilled salmon "De Salvo" or the bouillabaisse at the Bistro at Hotel Maison de Ville, on Toulouse. Of the crabmeat maison at Galatoire's. Of the pan-fried sheepshead at Peristyle. Of the salmon in tarragon beurre blanc with virtually ephemeral fried oysters and bits of leek preceded by fried green tomatoes with remoulade sauce, or, indeed, the grits and grillades, at Upperline. Of the truffled eggs at Bacco. Of the simple but savory beef brisket at Tujague's (pronounced Two-Jacks) on Decatur. Of the smoked trout dumplings or the seared foie gras with duck confit at Emeril's. Of the cane-smoked salmon at Commander's Palace, in the Garden District. Of the lavishly saucy barbecue shrimp at Mr. B's Bistro. Of a great grilled veal chop with caramelized shallot butter at Sbiza's, which on Sunday offers a fine jazz brunch. Of the triggerfish with truffle and cauliflower vinaigrette puree and asparagus and prosciutto chips at Bayona, on Dauphine, topped off by some kind of little coconut cookie that gives you hope, when you least expect it, that even in New Orleans there is always something more to learn about what taste buds are for. In New Orleans, people know chefs like Susan Spicer (Bayona, Herbsaint) or Ann Kearney (Peristyle) or Greg Piccolo (Bistro at Hotel Maison de Ville) or of course Emeril Lagasse (Emeril's) and restaurateurs, like JoAnn Clevenger of Upperline or the Brennans of Mr. B's and many other places, the way people know Jack Nicholson in Hollywood. And when was the last time Jack Nicholson made you think, "Oh, Jesus. Oh, Jesus. That is *good*"?

But you can't live like that. After a week in New Orleans trying to squeeze in all the cuisine you can, you wake up thinking, "With roux my heart is laden. If only a serpent would come along and tempt me with an apple."

No such luck. Satan is saying, "You know, Uglesich's is open. And they say the old man is getting tired and the son doesn't want to take over. How would you feel if Uglesich's were to close before you got back in town?" So at 11:30 a.m. I'm at this dump of a place on Baronne at Erato, a no-man's-land uptown of the Central Business District, girding my loins for what may be the best food in town.

Pronounced "Yoogle-sitches." A Yugoslav-American family. The place is so popular with local people, including other restaurants' chefs, that if you don't get there early for lunch you might have to wait three times: outside in line till you get through the door and reach the counter to order, then inside for a table, and then for your food. But nothing's expensive, and oh is it rich. Shrimp creole—"cooked," according to the menu, "with every tomato product you can imagine." Pan-fried trout topped with "muddy water" sauce: chicken broth, garlic, anchovies, and gutted jalapeños, and sprinkled with parmesan cheese. Fried green tomatoes with remoulade sauce. In Uglesich's I have felt, at times, that I was mopping up the most delicious grease I have ever put in and around my mouth, and that is saying something.

You don't have to pay much money to eat well in New Orleans. Turn most any corner in the Quarter and you will see a sign that says FOOD STORE, and inside will be crawfish egg rolls. That were made this morning. That are good. Peoples Grocery at Conti and Bourbon, the Royal

Street Grocery at St. Ann, the Verti Mart at Royal and Gov. Nicholls. You can get convenience-store fare, odds-and-ends items, newspapers, but you can also get California and French wines, liquor, black-eyed peas, gumbo, fried fish, crab cakes, jambalaya, red beans and rice, full breakfasts and all kinds of po-boys and regular sandwiches to order.

On Decatur between Dumaine and St. Philip, you can home in on the Italian influence. At Central Grocery, the muffaletta was invented: on a big round sesame-seed bun, slices of several different aromatic meats and cheeses and oily-garlicky olive salad. Half a muffaletta is enough, and then you can browse among imported pastas, spices, salamis, and canned goods including baby conch, quail eggs, octopus in oil, abalone mushrooms, Creole chow-chow, and Cajun trinity (onion, bell pepper, and celery).

I recommend the croissants at the Croissant d'Or, on Ursulines between Royal and Chartres. Or you can go to Johnny's Po-Boy on St. Louis, where the mule-carriage drivers and the living statues eat, and have red beans and rice or a bowl of gumbo or a Po-Boy sandwich, which you might call a hero or a sub, but in New Orleans it will contain things into which you can sink heroically. At Mother's, another unpricey place just uptown from Canal, you can have a roast beef sandwich with *debris,* which is the gravy and breakage you get when you roast beef slowly with, it goes without saying, seasoning.

"They don't have any seasoning up there," a cabdriver told me, in reference to everywhere north of New Orleans. "Nowhere knows about seasoning but here."

Then there is the whole area of fried chicken. "My mama didn't cook any cacciatore, or any pad Thai," says my friend Lolis Elie, the *Picayune* columnist. "But my mama fried chicken, so I know." Lolis will send you to the famous Dooky Chase, on Orleans, or to Willie Mae's, on St. Ann (both in the Treme district, across Rampart from the Quarter). The fried chicken at those places does make it clear that he was brought up right. But Jacques-Imo's on Oak Street, uptown, will serve you some fried chicken, which for juicy and yet not heavy is phenomenal, and you should also try the alligator cheesecake there—I know it sounds strange, but it is I think (and it's not sweet, now, don't let the word "cheesecake" put you off) the best way in the world to get some alligator in your system. Jacques-Imo's is also a friendly, talk-inducing place for a few drinks. Lay down a foundation of that alligator cheesecake (yes, it is rich, I didn't say it wasn't rich, but it's not show-off rich) and you are not going to get prematurely tipsy, I'll tell you that.

But my mama's fried chicken on the spectrum of juicy was more toward the chewy side than the succulent, and she didn't season it at all heavily, just brought the brown and the flesh into a balance that echoes down through my years. I have had chicken that reminded me of that chicken in a place on Frenchmen Street in the Faubourg

Marigny called The Praline Connection. From nearby tables you can overhear the unmistakable tones of reality-facing progressive biracial political palaver, and unless prices have gone up you can have crowder peas and okra and rice for five dollars, or with meat for $6.95. The meat might be chicken or it might be pork chops or something. And the fried okra—hot and lightly cornmealed, so that the okra, still holding its own in there, is a first-rate fusion of brown and green, to which you might want to add just a touch of red· hot sauce.

And there is a ramshackle-looking place across from the French Market called Fiorella's where not long ago I got three pieces of chicken with macaroni and cheese and vegetable du jour and a side of olive salad (chopped olives, pimientos, and spices) for $6.95. And my sweetheart, Joan, had the same. At the next table, only the woman was into it. "You're going to eat *turnip greens*?" the man said. "Sure am," she said. "I'm in New Orleans. Can't eat turnip greens in Davenport, Iowa." Excellent turnip greens, too. One waitress had tattoos all up and down both arms and was wearing a lacy black low-cut top, a short denim skirt, and a wholesome-sexy-friendly smile. The other one was putting on being grumpy, so some regulars could rag her into smiling.

"This is that *home* cooking," said one of the regulars.

"Huh," said the grumpy-looking waitress. "You ain't never been in no home."

In Fiorella's you could hear a street band playing

outside: a beat-up old tuba, a clarinet, a trumpet, a drum with cymbals, and a man singing a song about taking an arm from an old armchair and a cork from an old wine bottle, and from a horse some hair, "put it all together and you get more lovin' than I ever get from you." Doesn't sound like a romantic song, I know, but it was that afternoon. At our table, we were both into it.

Way up into the Bywater area on Chartres is a homey neighborhood place, Elizabeth's, whose motto is "Real Food. Done Real Good." Great breakfasts, and lunches whose sides include the mirliton, a green, pear-shaped vegetable sort of like a bell pepper, which I have never seen on a menu outside of New Orleans. But by now you may be stuffed. Before you get to Elizabeth's, you might want to linger along a certain block of Chartres. It's the block between two cross streets whose names enable you to say that you spent some time suspended between Piety and Desire.

Linger for say about a minute. And then if you're like me you start thinking of New Orleans as a woman who is sultry and tolerant and always feeds you great. And it's good-bye, Piety.

LAGNIAPPE WITH FOOD

The Italian influence

The Progresso soup company derives from members of the Taormina and Uddo families who came to New

Orleans from Sicily in the early 1900s. I once heard
Michael Uddo, formerly chef of the lamented G&E
Courtyard Grill, tell how immigrants would arrive from
Palermo in the nineteenth century carrying lemons and
spices in their pockets. "My grandmother was something
of a battle-ax," Uddo said, "so her father gave a dowry of
two tickets to America, and spent my grandparents' wedding night in their cabin so my grandfather wouldn't jump
ship." When the grandfather arrived in New Orleans, he
found that the Italian community couldn't find decent
tomato sauce anywhere in the country, so he made it,
packaged it in cans he rescued from the garbage, and delivered it door to door. Then he bought a donkey that
knew, from previous employment, the way to all the
wholesale groceries in the city.

Ramble Six: Desire

My woman do somethin', hon,
I never seen.
She must be goin'
With a man from New Orleans.

—FROM "CHITTLIN' SUPPER,"
BY PEG LEG HOWELL AND JIM HILL

*B*ACK WHEN THE U.S. WAS MORE GENERALLY PURI-
tanical, New Orleans was, as Faulkner wrote in
Absalom, Absalom!, "that city foreign and paradoxical, with
an atmosphere at once fatal and languorous . . . whose
denizens had created their All-Powerful and His supporting
hierarchy-chorus of beautiful saints and handsome angels in
the image of their houses and personal ornaments and
voluptuous lives," where the sophisticated Creole Charles
Bon tries to corrupt earnest Henry Sutpen into believing it
is honorable to keep an octoroon quasi-wife on the side.

These days in America as a whole, when the pig-ugly if heroic porn star Ron Jeremy tours Disneyland as a VIP and is mobbed by families wanting to take their picture with him, sex may have been run into the ground. In New Orleans it remains one of various things the air is pungent with. Couples come here for it. In the morning you see them out on the balconies, leaning against the ironwork, looking fond and frowsy. And they head back home having had a lot of it—there go two healthy young folks now, yawning and nudging each other as they pull wheeled suitcases past the strip joint on Bourbon where the sign says "Wash the Girl of Your Choice." (So the statement by Blanche DuBois, "The cathedral bells. That is the only clean thing in the Quarter," no longer holds up.)

Also arguing couples, to be sure. But I'm walking along Royal at nine-thirty of a fine Friday morning in October, and coming the other way on the other side of the street are two head-shaven guys and between them a pretty woman with long black switchy hair, I'd say late twenties, early thirties, I don't know, I can't tell anymore, they're all way younger than me. It's hard for three people to walk side by side on a New Orleans banquette, in fact that is a distinctive thing about walking in the Quarter: you can't just stream past people with no notice, you have to step over and squeeze past, and you pass residents on their front steps so close that it's socially awkward not to nod hello. So these three are sort of jostling, sportively, in the effort to keep all abreast. And here, from clear across the street, is what I hear the woman say:

"My hole hurts!"

She's walking funny, as though she means it, but the three of them chuckle, a little hoarsely.

"Boo-hoo," she adds.

They seem to be friends of some standing. They're not showing off, it's nine-thirty in the morning, there's hardly anybody around and they're not even implicitly cutting their eyes over at me. You might prefer *Jules et Jim* angst, and no doubt the relationship won't always remain so unvexed, but I'd say they've been up all night and they're bushed but jolly. A few more words pass among the three that I can't hear and then, she:

"All I know is, my hole hurts!"

And they go briskly on along. People are still coming to New Orleans to do things they wouldn't back home.

As for myself—you're going to be disappointed to hear this, but I have not done anything in New Orleans that you wouldn't have done, if you had been there at the time. Anyway I can't imagine why you wouldn't have. Well there was this one Super Bowl week back in the seventies when Pete Axthelm of *Newsweek* and I both took an interest in a flower vendor named Molly who was barefoot and dressed in a chenille-bedspread toga, and we bought all her flowers and walked around the Quarter the three of us playing kazoos and then went to my room in the Marriott, which had two big beds in it, and as soon as she had washed her feet and we had shown her some identification, so she could be sure we had been telling her the true stories of our lives, Molly had the run of the place. It was nice. She expressed the hope that this gambol, as she put it, would get her nerve up to tell her boyfriend Leonard of her plans to move to New Zealand and become a shepherdess. In the morning I gave her a Super Bowl ticket, but as best I could make out from friends who sat in the same section, she must have passed it on to a small, edgy man, maybe Leonard, who once, when Fran Tarkenton evaded a headlong Steeler rush (not that it got him anywhere), said, "Never try to horse a soft-mouthed fish."

When it comes to vice, I am not your best reporter. Vice to me is like corruption and bad television: it's appealing if it's *period* vice. You might think that New Orleans amounts to a perpetually period town, but no. Even in New Orleans, from what I can gather, contemporary vice is like contemporary so many other things: political rhetoric, for instance. Over-determined. Prophylactic to a fault.

In 1854 in New Orleans a local man told Frederick Law Olmsted that New England boys who had been "too carefully brought up at home" frequently came to New Orleans and sank into degradation. When I, who had been brought up carefully enough in Georgia that it might almost have been in New England, spent my twenty-first summer in New Orleans, in 1963, I kept a diary. "I am going to have to tell the folks that I like beer," I confided. "I still hate the idea of cocktail parties and hope I always do, but I now of-ficially drink beer, and I'm not going to sneak around about it. I hope." I had a ways to go, to come out of my shell. In a strip joint, I chatted with "one of those B-girls I'd heard so much about," but when the establishment tried to charge me four-fifty for her beer, I could honestly say that after paying $1.50 for my beer (which struck me as a ripoff) I had three dollars to my name. So she got up and danced, and I noted what seemed to be a bee tattooed on her shoul-der, and then she sat back down next to me.

> *I asked her how long she'd been in this business and she said fifty years and I said she probably wasn't even that old and she said no a year and a half. "Was that a bee?" I asked. Couldn't see it now because she had on a little kimono thing.*
>
> *"Mm hm," she said, and shrugged her shoulder so I could just see it. "But if you don't have any more money for us, I guess I better go sit over there all by myself in the corner."*
>
> *And she did. But was nice about it. When I left to call E. [Ellen, my college girlfriend, who was off working as a camp counselor, and whom I would marry a year later], she waved affectionately.*

Maybe I read too much into the wave, but it did seem a bit like lagniappe. Here from my diary are two more experiences:

Experience No. 1, in no particular order: I interviewed Miss Universe. Very impressive young lady, Argentinian, learned English just by talking to people since she became Miss U. last year, very beautiful. She was obviously above the whole silly business of being mistress to the Universe and above the aging charm boys she was surrounded by. I tried to record that in my story, don't know if I did, sent it to E., E. doesn't think so.

Experience No. 2, I ran into Nigel Begg, now known as Tony Begg, as I was sitting in front of a laundromat waiting for my clothes to dry. He is from Scotland, was in high school with me, kicked off the track team for being a Communist, though nobody took him seriously. He supposedly swallowed a nickel once to impress people. Anyway he's working in a warehouse and going to art school at night. Writing poetry, too. He asked me if I read much, I said yes, so we've gotten together several times and discussed things. He knows Nietzsche and has read almost all of Dostoyevsky. Says he figured out evolution before he read Darwin, anyway has an ontology worked out. Now says he's an anarchist. I went with him to art school one night, mostly to satisfy a lifelong desire to see a nude model, it must be confessed, and I saw one. She kept glaring at me. I concentrated most of my attention on the other artists, but she asked me finally if I painted, and I replied with abominable heartiness no I was just visiting, and she put on her robe and refused to pose until I left. So I did, but pausing at the door to look

at something on the wall so as to have a simulacrum of
poise. But she was right, I am not an artist.

I lost touch with Nigel, or Tony, after that. I guess I
embarrassed him. But I am more a man of the world today.
One night recently, feeling I owed it to you, I ventured
into a "gentlemen's club" on Bourbon called Temptations.
Kenneth Holditch, the Tennessee Williams scholar who
takes people on literary tours of the Quarter, had told me
it was once the mansion of Judah P. Benjamin, known outside the Confederacy as "the brains of the Confederacy."
Benjamin served for most of the war as Confederate secre-
tary of state and, after the war, was sharp enough to escape
by way of the West Indies to England. He was not the balls
of the Confederacy. When after ten years of marriage his
beautiful, notoriously flirtatious Creole wife got pregnant,
people said it was by some other man. Then she took off to
Paris with the baby and had many open affairs, which she
would flaunt when he visited her there, to see the child.
Now his parlor has come to this: desultory down-to-thong
stripping, and over in one corner a guy getting a lap dance.
She's in a crouch like a baseball catcher, facing him.

Call me cranky, but I don't see a lap dance's allure. Talk
about contemporary. A strange strapping woman in a
thong hunkered over your loins, pinning you down, grind-
ing away, purpose being I suppose to make you come in
your pants? Or would that be out of line? Once I was getting a haircut in Head Quarters on Dauphine. In the lap of

the man in the next chair was a big black and white cat. I asked whether there was a cat for me, but my barber said this was not standard lagniappe: "This man has been coming in here for years, and this is the first time Dickie's jumped up in his lap." The man was stroking Dickie gingerly. "And I'm not a cat person," he said. Dickie's tail was twitching, but he was purring or at least close to purring until the man said, "He's so happy," whereupon Dickie bit him, hard, and jumped down. As if to say, "Who are you to tell a cat he's happy?"

To me this lap dance looks like an even less nearly mutual experience than that. From the point of view of the old boy having his groin ground, well, not that he came in there to show poise (though I'll bet he slapped on a little cologne), but still. Dry-humping—though no substitute for wet-humping, particularly in New Orleans—is one thing, but *being dry-humped,* and apparently not being allowed any use of the hands (except for occasional incidental contact while he's trying to think what to do with them), he might as well be a fish. This, to me, is not getting your hambone boiled. And it is so not cuddling.

From the lap dancer's point of view, well, she is on top. But on top of what? Together they resemble an etching of a succubus at work on some poor soul. Is that the same lap that this guy's children sit on?

Another sex worker, I guess is the term, comes up to me, with a little leopard-skin thing wrapped around her, and says, "You look like you're trouble in a box."

Right. There's a *noir* title for you. But probably the person in the box would not be the protagonist. I'm trying to frame a *noir* denial when the lap dancer walks by, pulling a little halter-top thing over her palpably (strike that) fake boobs, and my girl (strike that) says to her, "What goes around comes around, *Jack*."

Inferrably, the lap dancer has stolen this last dance, but I have never heard a woman call another woman "Jack" before, in that tone of voice. I chug my $7.50 beer (in constant dollars, probably about the same price as the one that cost me $1.50 back in 1963), mutter my excuses, and go out into the night.

Just up the street is Larry Flynt's Hustler Club. One of those electronic crawl signs out front. It says, "Welcome Federation of Societies for Coatings Technology Coatings." Looks like an excess of *Coatings*'s, maybe something Freudian there, but let it go.

Nearby on Bourbon, and right next door to Galatoire's, the most venerably distinguished restaurant in town, a shop calls itself "Bourbon-Strip Tease, Lingerie and Adult Gifts." It offers turkey-feather halters, teddies with nipple-holes on either side of the red-letter exclamation HEY BABY, glow-in-the-dark fingerpaints, "Pecker Party Lights," and at least two inflatable items, a Tartan jockstrap sort of affair and a "party sheep."

Period vice had to be better, even at the time. Until World War I, when the federal government shut it down so it wouldn't corrupt the navy, there was a neighborhood just north of the Quarter called Storyville, which comprised well over a hundred whorehouses. There's a wonderful book by Al Rose called *Storyville, New Orleans, Being an Authentic, Illustrated Account of the Notorious Red-Light District,* in which we learn that in some of these houses, dances were danced that were "so abandoned and reckless," according to a contemporary account, "that the can-can in comparison seemed maidenly and respectable." Perhaps one of these was the "ham kick," in which a ham was hung from the ceiling, several feet off the floor. Any woman who managed to kick it could have the ham, as long as she wasn't wearing underdrawers. In nicer establishments, patrons could do the fox-trot with naked women. In Emma Johnson's house, a woman known as Olivia, the Oyster Dancer, performed as follows:

> *Completely naked, she began by placing a raw oyster on her forehead and then leaned back and "shimmied" the oyster back and forth over her body without dropping it, finally causing it to run down to her instep, from which a quick kick would flip it high in the air, whereon she would catch it on her forehead where it started. An aged prostitute assured the author . . . that this was now "a lost art."*

That is a dance I would pay to see. For one thing, if you're going to shimmy an oyster all over you, you're going to have to get pretty moist yourself, otherwise that oyster is going to dry up and drop off, reduced to how a chicken liver gets when it's floured to be fried, or worse, like a slug when it's salted. Olivia flourished before air-conditioning. One night in New Orleans recently I attended a performance at the Shim-Sham Club, which is tongue-in-cheek burlesque, which may sound redundant, but in this day and age, that is the way to take burlesque. It's a show for couples, featuring "the three R's, wrigglin', writhin' and razzmatazz." The bumps and grinds are retro-spicy, as are the jokes: "She so enjoyed her coming-out party, she hasn't been home since," and "She puts the *t* and *a* in 'teacher's assistant,' " and "A gambling man said, 'I'll lay you ten to one.' I said, 'It's an odd time, but I'll be there.' "

The Shim-Sham dancers control the medium without sitting on anybody. But none of them will go down in history, like Olivia. After the show, Kitty West, who danced in the fifties as Evangeline the Oyster Girl, was autographing pictures of herself in her prime. Her specialty's oyster connection was just that she emerged from a big shell. "And you want to know a secret?" she said to me. "I don't even like oysters." I believe that Olivia did like them.

Emma Johnson herself offered her "sixty-second plan": any man who could delay his orgasm for as long as a minute inside her, didn't have to pay. Once in a while, she would let somebody win. Emma staged sex "circuses" in her parlor. Rose interviews a woman, a respectable mother and grandmother, "a plump housewife who speaks in distinctively New Orleans tones," whose husband knows her past: she was born and reared in Emma's. When she was "getting a little figure," she began to perform in the circuses, with her mother. "She's the one who used to fuck the pony," she says. "And in the daytime me and Liz [another "trick baby" like herself] *rode* the ponies around the yard. . . . Ain't *that* somethin'?"

The words right out of my mouth. One of Rose's sources was a genteel woman who came to New Orleans in 1896 after she was marginally, even virginally, touched by scandal and her father told her never to darken his door again. She found employment, solely administrative, in one of the nicer houses. She told Rose that King Carol of Rumania attended one of Emma's circuses, though she was not sure he was king yet at the time.

I doubt you'd bump into a prince at a New Orleans vice den today. In 2002 there was a big story by Michael Perlstein in the *Times-Picayune* about the federal busting of an "infamous Canal Street brothel" that I had not heard of. The madam, Jeanette Maier, disclosed that she had been a victim of so much child abuse that she "began to feel detached from her own body." Her mother helped her run the place, and her daughter was charged with turning tricks there. The daughter said, "The women in our family are strong and beautiful, but they're cursed." The story was accompanied by a color photo of the three of them posing rather jauntily. They'd all been abused from an early age, by uncles, by at least one nun. . . . Their brothel had "rugs and mirrors from Pottery Barn."

More tasteful than the pony thing. But the old houses,

the high-end ones at least, were all marble, mahogany, mirrors, brocade, and Tiffany chandeliers. And women with so-here-they-are bodies and faraway eyes, judging from the famous photographs by Ernest J. Bellocq. Orphans, probably, in one sense or another.

One evening on Bourbon Street, a vision caught my eye. I was walking past an open-to-the-street bar where a band was playing "Proud Mary" and patrons were dancing. A golden-blond woman, evidently naturally buxom and lily-fair and untanned all over, in a bright white string bikini, was rolling, rolling, rolling on the river with whatever fellow proffered the right size bill, I guess, because she had money tucked into her outfit's virtually nonexistent white-spiderweb top. Ample though she was, and "ample" is an insufficient term, she looked so much lighter than the prevailing humidity that she bordered on being afloat. She appeared to be enjoying herself thoroughly. A mounted policeman in the street crooked his finger to get her out of there. She ignored him, kept on dancing, lots of wobble syncopated with the flow. The cop sighed, got down from his horse, and—he couldn't see what happened, I couldn't see what happened, the horse, too, looked surprised—she was gone. As if in a dream. Maybe she was inflated, somebody pulled a stopper and she went *pfflluuh*. If not, she probably came from an abusive background, too. Bring somebody you want *with* you to New Orleans, is my recommendation.

LAGNIAPPE WITH DESIRE

HENRY SUTPEN

Faulkner himself in New Orleans, when he was twenty-seven, swathed his small-town Mississippi self in lies about war wounds. Said he had a steel plate in his head. Made a point of dressing bohemian, for instance in an enormous overcoat with inner pockets that held several half-gallon jars of corn liquor. Sherwood Anderson, who gave him formative guidance and encouragement, told someone that Faulkner in that coat reminded him of Lincoln's remark about Alexander Stephens, the diminutive vice-president of the Confederacy: "Did you ever see so much shuck for so little nubbin?" Perhaps that remark got back to Faulkner, who went on not only to outwrite Anderson a hundredfold but also to lampoon him in a book called *Sherwood Anderson and Other Creoles.*

STORYVILLE

Sidney Story, an anti-vice alderman of New Orleans, put through the legislation that confined the city's prostitution to that area. To his dismay, the press began referring to the district as Storyville, and the name caught on in the street. The designator signified by the designated.

In *Buddy Bolden and the Last Days of Storyville,* Danny Barker tells of the famously soft-spoken pimp Clerk Wade, who escorted all his sporting women—except for one,

Angelina, who had not fulfilled her weekly quota—to a ball at the Roof Garden, to hear King Oliver's band and get some fresh air. Angelina went alone to the Big Twenty-Five club, where she sobbed and drank absinthe until daylight, when Clerk and the rest of his stable rolled in. Clerk went to her booth to console her in his dulcet-toned way and have a pork-chop sandwich. Angelina took a pistol from her purse and shot him five times in the chest. He fell to the floor, his shirtfront on fire from the muzzle blast. His last words were a whisper: "Li'l girl, I'm sorry I did not take you to the ball." After she told the police her side of it, she was released.

According to Al Rose's book, some women in the Storyville district "stood on sidewalks in kimonos, which they would flash open now and then to display their bodies." Compare the recollection of Stephanie Dupuy, who in the sixties attended a private girls' school on Prytania Street: "We'd be sitting out front wearing little miniskirts, and cars would go by, and the old biddies would come out and say, 'Backs to Prytania, girls!' "

Naked dancing

Jelly Roll Morton, who wrote a tune called "The Naked Dance," told Alan Lomax that naked dancing in New Orleans was "a real art," particularly in the house run by Gypsy Schaeffer, "one of the most notoriety women I have ever seen in a high-class way. She was the notoriety kind that everybody liked." A great piano player ("professors" they were called in the houses) named Tony Jackson held forth there. He wrote the song "Pretty Baby." Although the movie *Pretty Baby* was inspired by Al Rose's Storyville book and tells the story of a whorehouse child, such nakedness as crops up in it is demure. If you ask my sweetheart and me, the most romantic movie scene involving the song "Pretty Baby" is in the 1935 classic *Ruggles of Red Gap.* "Nell's place," in the western mining town of Red Gap, is not a house of ill repute, it is just a place where folks who aren't snooty can go to drink a bit and have a good time. When a visiting earl (Roland Young) stops in there and meets Nell (Leila Hyams), there is no nudity, certainly, but there is a definite spark. "Do you believe in love at first sight?" she asks him with a worldly twinkle in her eye. "No," he says in an unassumingly suave, upper-crust mumble, "that's why I thought I'd stay awhile." As Nell sings "Pretty Baby" at the piano, she teaches the earl to provide accompaniment, "ditta-boom," on a drum set. In the end he takes her back to England to be his wife. Couldn't there be a place like Nell's place with naked dancing?

Do not confuse that engaging earl with the stuffy Creole gent, also played by Roland Young, who woos Marlene Dietrich in *Flame of New Orleans* (1941). Adventuress though she means to be, she dumps this rich fellow for knockabout boat captain Bruce Cabot. No spark there. Nor in *New Orleans,* which was originally conceived by Orson Welles as Louis Armstrong playing himself in his life story and the story of jazz. Such a movie could have gone some way toward connecting jazz with the word's original use as a verb meaning to have carnal knowledge, since Pops enjoyed a hearty and sometimes hair-raising love life in New Orleans—"right *amongst* all this vice," as he jauntily recalled—and points north. However, the project fell into other hands and devolved into a tepidly romantic semimusical in which Armstrong and Billie Holiday—playing a maid, in her only feature-film appearance—are relegated to asexual margins by white persons of drastically lesser erotic charge. The sexiest New Orleans movie scene, to my knowledge, is Ellen Barkin and Dennis Quaid going at it heatedly and convincingly, with their clothes mostly on, in *The Big Easy,* which gave the city a new nickname. Otherwise, unless you go for the bloodless Tom Cruise in *Interview with a Vampire,* New Orleans movies have been less libidinous than the sign outside a dry-cleaning establishment in the Quarter: DROP YOUR PANTS AT ARABI CLEANERS.

Well, the relationship chat, woman to husband, between Barbara Bel Geddes and Richard Widmark at the end of *Panic in the Streets* is pretty hot in a marital way. Especially if you can't help thinking of her just a little bit as Miss Ellie and him as Tommy Udo, who pushed the old lady down the stairs. Oh, is she slick in the way she slips it to him that he's a lucky guy because they're going to have another baby, when they can hardly afford the child they have. Slick in a way that's good for all of them.

Ramble Seven: Friends

If ifs was skiffs, we'd all be boating.

—NEW ORLEANS EXPRESSION

AN OYSTER IS HERMAPHRODITIC. ONCE IT SURVIVES the floating, shell-less larval stage, and until we wrench it out of the only home it's ever known, an oyster doesn't have to go anywhere, even to reproduce. So it doesn't. Unlike the questing and burrowing clam, an oyster has virtually no foot, which is why it goes down so easy.

What Tennessee Williams called "a certain flexible quality in my sexual nature" would appear to go down easily in the Quarter. Storefront signs proclaim enterprises called Mary Hardware, the Nelly Deli, Queen Fashion ("Masks! They're not just for the bedroom anymore. Halloween is around the corner"), Flora Savage (a florist apparently specializing in wildflowers), and the Crow Bar, which is what it takes to separate the men from the boys.

At the Clover Grill on Bourbon, which never closes, you can get a good eggs-bacon-and-grits breakfast or a hamburger "cooked under an American-made hubcap," to quote the menu, which is saucy: "Clover Weenie, a quarter pound of pure beef pleasure (select staff members available for private parties)." There always seem to be at least three men behind the counter, engaging in gay badinage:

"Someone in the group—"

"Did I hear my name?"

"Is your name 'Someone in the group'?"

"Just checking. I don't want no drama."

"Oh, I do. What else is there?"

"Miss Ma'am, there are ladies here—do something for them."

"Get away! I'm singing 'Sea of Love.' "

Which is playing on the jukebox voted the best in the Quarter. Everything romantic from Lauren Hill to the B-52s.

" 'Come with me . . .' That's my favorite part."

"You queen."

"I still have a living mother. Address me as 'Princess.' "

Then "Keep Your Head to the Sky," by Earth, Wind & Fire, comes on, and everybody behind the counter is singing along and dancing, and then "Oh Happy Day, When Jesus Washed My Sins Away," and everybody in the place joins in.

Except for my high-school English teacher, Ann Lewis, I never had a literary friend, even through four years of college, until the summer I spent in New Orleans when I was twenty-one. I met Matthew Snow in the Quarter, in the Jazz Museum, which isn't there anymore. He was originally from Gainesville, Georgia. When he heard I was from the same state, he said he'd show me around and introduce me to people. He was thirty-one. He limped and spoke haltingly as a result of a car crash, after which, he said, he heard a doctor pronounce him dead. He had taught philosophy at NYU, he said. He said he had met James Thurber and Jonathan Winters and knew Plaquemines Parish boss Leander Perez and the late Earl Long's widow, Miz Blanche. He said he had studied under Robert Penn Warren, Thornton Wilder, Frank Lloyd Wright, and *with* Norman Mailer under André Gide's son, or brother, or maybe it was Gide himself. He said he had filed sheet music for Toscanini. He said he knew five languages (I heard him speak fluently in German and French) and people at *The New Yorker*. He had a great apartment on Bourbon. I wrote in my diary:

He's self-conscious and shy, and strange, so we have trouble, given my undemonstrativeness and willingness to drift, getting along very naturally, but I hope we can have an interesting friendship. I feel a little bit apprehensive about taking up with such a mysterious person, but it's

about time I started meeting people on a purely human
basis, not as classified fellow workers or students.

We walked the streets of New Orleans—he gimpily
but gamely—talking about the arts for hours on end. He
got me into the last club I ever belonged to: the Thompson's Club. It gathered in Thompson's Cafeteria on St.
Charles late every night to drink coffee and talk. There
was Babe, a former prizefighter and former cabdriver who
was said to be "living off a chicken farm," and told stories
that I had a hard time following except for one about a little girl actress in Hollywood who got paid three hundred
dollars a week, "and she didn't have to do anything but
smile, and she wouldn't smile, so her mother had to beat
her to get her to smile."

Mrs. Leslie, the fiftyish widow of a policeman, plump
and not averse to marrying again, as she made plain by
saying "My husband, God rest his soul," frequently.
Matthew loved to listen to her stories, which consisted almost entirely of explaining who everybody in them was:
"He was the middle one, who jumped off the levee. The
old one is the one who used to live next door to me and
would put on a wig and a bonnet and a pipe and entertain
me through the window. You know, he was quite good.
He was a busboy for a while and then he was a boxer and
his family did everything they could to get him to go to
church, and when he did he just sat there."

Armand and Toots Hug, he the accomplished but not

very ambitious pianist in one of the clubs, quiet and suave-looking in a nice sort of way, in his fifties, and she disintegrating from dipsomania, not quite all there in a charming, almost, way, patting her husband's hand until, without making any sign of irritation, he would withdraw it.

Dutch, a typesetter at the *Times-Picayune,* who described the place, with little rancor, as a salt mine, and would stop eating every now and then to remark, "I think I could eat if my throat was cut."

Pink Earmuffs, as he was called because he came in wearing some one night and looked at himself in the mirror, carefully. He let drop that he wanted to buy a continent—New Zealand, maybe. He operated an ice-cream cart, the kind you pedal like a huge tricycle, and always wore a checked shirt, a suit, and a bow tie.

Full of characters, New Orleans! During working hours at the *Times-Picayune* I was shown a photograph (from the front) of former governor Earl Long, during his crazy period, taking a dump out a window of the Roosevelt Hotel, and I met a wizened woman of the Quarter who made and sold fruitcakes and also played the horses. A socially prominent lady ordered several hundred dollars' worth of fruitcakes for a lavish tea party she was giving, and made the mistake of paying in advance. On the day of the party, the hostess put in a frantic call to the fruitcake lady: "My guests are all here, and the liquor is here—where are the fruitcakes?"

"Drink up, Doilin'," said the fruitcake lady. "The fruitcakes come in third."

Not vice but *characters,* that's what I wanted. Bumpy Doucet, the assistant city editor, told me of the legendary crack reporter Walter Goodstein, who went with a photographer to interview the French bombshell Corrine Calvet "at 9:00 a.m. in her hotel room," according to my diary, "and came back drunk with the photographer at 4:30 p.m. after having raised all manner of hell with her, getting her picture in the shower and being convivial in various ways he never would tell anybody about." Nope. Not a word.

I wanted to be a crack reporter.

However, I was sort of semi-engaged to be married, and not very outgoing. I went with Matthew to visit an artist named Lorraine. It startled me to hear her say she was in love with a man who was involved with another man, and she didn't like it when the three of them went out together. I was even more startled to hear that this was just the second time she had met Matthew. People opened up to Matthew quickly, but I didn't know how to take him, as I told my diary:

Why can't I have simple associations with people? Matthew isn't sure I want him around, and I'm not sure he's what he seems to be, or exactly what it is that he seems to be. He showed me a piece he wrote on Kafka that

*seemed pretty good though loaded down with Freudian
terms. He says he's decided he's not a writer, that he'd be
a teacher if he could talk better—he doesn't stutter exactly,
it's more an intermittent struggle to get his thought out—
but as it is he doesn't know what to do.*

Matthew shared my enthusiasm, which has since
cooled, for the characters of J. D. Salinger, who were hu-
morous, brilliant, appalled by phoniness, and always verg-
ing on spiritual crisis. He reminded me of Zooey, I told
my diary:

*He's always prodding me along nicely by asking embar-
rassing questions about what I've read or said and by
leaving me notes in German. I'm not used to friendship
so intense, sudden and straightforward. I feel like the
farmer who, when the man from the Department of
Agriculture told him he could farm better using modern
methods, said he wasn't farming half as good as he could,
right now.*

Matthew had recuperated from his accident at a monastery in Conyers, Georgia. One of the monks there had
been a good companion for him, he said, because he had
accepted Matthew as Christopher Robin. He left me a
poignant little note, a conversation between Winnie the
Pooh and C.R., with W. getting bored and losing interest

after the two of them plan to do something together, or suspecting that there is a catch to it somewhere. ("W: It's free? C: Yes, it's free. W: I don't know.")

What can I tell you? *Winnie the Pooh* was one of the primary texts via which my mother taught me to read. Okay? And I still had a soft spot for it. I guess so did Matthew. (But he also turned me on to Bessie Smith.) And I "maintained," as I told my diary, "that Pooh and C.R. were more casual than that. It doesn't seem right to me to be that dedicated and sympathetic and close to anybody, especially a man, that I have known so briefly and have been through so little with. Several hours later he said he decided he didn't know how to be a friend. He turned away and said he'd be friends on my terms."

A few days later, he proved that the Thompson's Club wasn't his only connection:

We went to visit Walker Percy yesterday, at his house in Covington. They have a mutual friend at the monastery. Percy was very hospitable, mild-looking but direct and relaxed and with impressive eyes. We sat around with him and his wife and two daughters, Mary Pratt, fifteen or sixteen, very sophisticated and conversant for her age, obviously used to participating in adult discussions, and Ann, seven or eight, who is deaf and whose talk is accordingly very hard to understand—she shot rubber-tipped arrows at the walls for a while as we talked. Their house is comfortable but not pretentious, with a small river in the backyard (they invited us to come water-skiing). He was disappointed when we didn't want a drink, though he'd heard that Matthew was a teetotaler. (Percy would be an alcoholic, he said, but for the fact he has a weak gut—he throws up after five drinks.) We had two or three cups of coffee, served by Mary P., who also lit her father's cigarettes and was said to be very obedient about dating and all. They were going to move her to a Catholic school in N.O. until they heard that the one in Covington was to be integrated, they want to support that so left her in.

They talked about Catholic matters, with occasional jocular reference to my heathenism. Matthew said the monks at Conyers can only speak with permission, so they express their dissatisfaction at something being read or performed at meals by crunching their celery loudly. Some of them enliven masses by posing as various Peanuts characters secretly and letting the others who are in on it guess who they are. They give hints surreptitiously by sign language. One of them plays the stock market, has built up an imaginary fortune, which makes him very independent.

We found to our pleasant surprise (M. had refused to read any more of Moviegoer after Binx Bolling said he didn't like the Quarter because of patio intellectuals and homosexuals; you can't just dismiss those people, M. says) that Percy likes the Quarter, has always wanted to live there, but Mrs. P. is afraid for her daughters on the *streets. I asked him how closely he identified with Binx and he said not at all. His "confessional" novels, he said, were fortunately too bad to be published. He said the only way you could ever start writing was to prove to yourself that you were unfit to do anything else, which made me feel a little better about my possible literary future. He sent* Moviegoer *to an agent, who took it straight to Knopf, who said they would publish it, but they didn't like the last half, which was intensely religious, full of abstruse conversations with priests, so he spent two years rewriting it, that half, and said he never did get it right.*

When Alfred Knopf read it he howled, didn't like it, had thought it was like Percy's uncle's book, Lanterns on the Levee, *but it was already out. Percy tried to give Mrs. Knopf some autographed copies of it, seemed to be the thing to do, but she said she didn't want any. All his Catholic New Orleans friends congratulated him on the book until they read it, then he didn't hear from them until a priest reviewed it favorably, when they congratulated him again. He didn't care much for* Catch-22, *although he thought it original, because Heller had a good idea but kept going on and on with it and didn't know what to do with it.*

Mrs. P. was smart-looking and intelligent, homey enough, too, blond and plumping up. Her father was there, almost totally disabled, mute, from a stroke. They have a terrier-Chihuahua that slept on everybody and

*barked at everybody. Percy said he writes for three hours
every morning, then quits.*

I was impressed by how respectfully Percy listened to
Matthew and sought his opinions. The Percys appreciated
as much as I did Matthew's story about a family whose
Chihuahua died. They put it in the deep freeze until they
could get it stuffed, then found out how much it cost to
stuff it, then just left it there because they couldn't bear to
thaw it out. But Matthew still confused me, I wrote a few
days later:

> *If he were a character in a novel, I would accept him as
> my alter ego and inspiration, but I just can't quite accept
> him as all that in the flesh. I can't take all this striving
> to relate and to give. It ain't natural. But he has awak-
> ened my interest in art, music ranging from opera to
> jazz, he has given me sermons on working and not let-
> ting things interfere and associating with the true and
> beautiful and avoiding the sleazy and superficial—he
> has stirred me to dedication. At least I think he has, but
> he's been with me so much I haven't had a chance to try
> my dedication out.*

I never got anywhere with the novel I'd been trying to
write. My parents and sister came to town for a few days. I
introduced Matthew to them, but he didn't say much, self-
conscious about his speech defect, I figured. My mother

said he seemed nice. I showed the folks around New Orleans and "we had a very happy time," according to my diary. My father displayed the sort of adult male behavior I was accustomed to: "They went shopping for antiques yesterday while I was at work, and Daddy went with them though they suggested he stay here and read since he wouldn't enjoy it, and he *didn't* enjoy it, obviously, and got tired, so they had to come back early."

My New Orleans diary ends with my parents' visit. I didn't write about the last time I saw Matthew. It was a sweltering August night, my last in town. I was relieved to be leaving there to see Ellen, my future wife, in Texas. Matthew and I had dinner, we walked back to my apartment, and as I was unlocking the door to the courtyard, he said, "Don't you *realize* that I feel affection for you, *physically*? Are you so insensitive, or naïve—"

Both. I went through the door and banged it shut, never looked back. The worst thing you could be, back home, was queer. I didn't even want to be, anyway. In Texas I got a letter from Matthew, saying he wanted to send a story I'd shown him (and which in fact was no good) to Caroline Gordon, the novelist and critic. If I wrote him back at all, it wasn't nicely. I told Ellen about it, how traumatic it had been for me. It didn't interest her much.

I told her I needed her (to reassure me, I guess), and she didn't like that at all. This confirmed my belief that outward need is counterproductive. I have erred in the other direction ever since. As far as I can tell. And every time I come to New Orleans I play that scene with Matthew back.

In my defense I could mention that he had referred to homosexuals, as if in sympathy, as "those people." But when he opened his heart, my reaction had not been even cryptically sympathetic, and let's just put it in professional terms: it is not a good idea for a writer to let himself get away with consigning anybody to any category of *those.*

When you get startled negatively, that bad energy stays with you until you use it either to lash out or to expand your sympathy. New Orleans is a place of exploration and masquerade, a place where a person can play roles, try on other identities. So okay, say I put myself in the place of a female student whose professor takes up a lot of time with her and suddenly puts his hand on her knee. I think, being her, *He doesn't think I'm smart, he just wants to get into my pants.*

No, this isn't working. In the first place, part of me is sympathizing with the professor already. He probably thinks you're smart (great, now I'm thinking of the female student as *you*) *and* he wants to get into your pants, the poor, aging dumpy son of a bitch. Not that I would ever do anything that out of line. But I can imagine how he feels. Show him you're smart, by moving your knee.

In the second place, what I tried to assume I would

think, if I were the student with the knee, is not what I thought. I was already guiltily weary of Matthew's intellectual attention. To realize that it was excessive, because semi-glandular, should have been a relief.

Wait. Now I *am* getting a flash of solidarity with the female student. Let's say you're me, okay, and I'm a woman whose knee *you* put a hand on, literally or figuratively but at rate not heavily (*you* think, because it's your hand), and I (the one with the knee) recoil. Well, jeez, she didn't have to *recoil,* you're probably thinking, and your hand is feeling like a rotten mackerel. At least that's what *I* would probably have been thinking, if the one with the hand had been me. But what *you're* feeling . . .

I can't keep track. So okay, here's how I felt: dumb. And preyed upon. It wasn't as if he'd said anything mean. But you know how you feel naked when you get a sense that somebody feels naked toward you. And you shudder a little, with appetite if you like it, with dread if you don't. Maybe everybody, not just oysters, is all morsel at heart. And I'm a guy, how would I know how to turn down sex politely?

Well, no. If Matthew had been a woman . . . Let's face it: here I am writing a book about New Orleans, and I have felt homophobia. I'll say this for me, I didn't like it.

But I can't mark it all down to horror of relationships in which you discuss the relationship. Over the years, of necessity, I have advanced to the point that I can have such a relationship, but not with men. With men, it's what I am tempted to call (in the sense that a song is higher than an affidavit), a higher level of communication: funny stories. Like the one about the three bulls who hear that a new bull is coming to the pasture and one of them says, "I got a dozen cows that are all mine, as you well know, and he ain't getting any of them."

Second bull says, "I got nine cows, and if he thinks he's touching a one of *them,* he's got another thing coming."

Third bull says, "Well, I got only the two, but they're mine and I'm keeping them."

Then the new bull arrives. He jumps out of the van and hits the ground snorting. He's big, he's black, he's rippling all over. He's looking around the pasture, getting ready to stake his claim.

"Well," says the first bull, "I do have more cows than I need, I reckon, and if he wants a few, you know . . ."

"I'm of that way of thinking, too, I believe," says the second bull. "No point in being too selfish."

The third bull starts snorting, bellowing, swelling up his chest, and pawing the dirt.

The first and second bull say, "Hey, whoa, what in the world are you doing? That new bull is going to see you."

"That's right," says the third bull, "and I want to be sure he knows I'm a bull."

Dread of gender-malleability. My friend Slick, in the twenty-five years I knew him, was burly, bearded, and hearty, a small-plane pilot and motorcycle racer at ease with firearms and in rough milieux. In his prime he appealed readily to adventurous women. We are speaking now of the seventies and early eighties, when Americans looked to Willie Nelson, not Donald Trump, as an exemplar of the good life. So I am not talking about weirdly sleek models who appear to have been turned out according to corporate guidelines—I'm talking about rowdy women of spirit who skinny-dip, suck crawfish heads (the only way to do justice to a mess of whole boiled ones), and appreciate George Jones. Slick knew at least two along those lines in New Orleans alone. One, in particular, who joined us one evening while we were working up to looking for orphans, let's call her Miranda. She was great looking without discernible makeup, she was funny, she loved oysters, she was earthy *and* sparkly, and she was a reader.

When I say *reader* I don't mean of books about whether there can ever be any truly emotional life anymore in the vacuum left by some lout who was her whole world and didn't have any feelings, himself, I mean real fiction, serious fiction: fiction *about* fiction. In New Orleans she had just been reading the Italo Calvino novel *If on a Winter's Night a Traveler*. Damn. Whereas Slick—now Slick was a reader himself, for a photographer, but Slick hadn't been reading Italo Calvino. I hadn't either, but I had read reviews of that Calvino novel and could have faked it. If Miranda had been severe and pale, reading Calvino would not have been a plus, but this woman— you figured you could take her anywhere, goat-roast or film festival, and she'd bring something welcome to the party. She actually quoted something from that novel that made my eyes go googly. Later I tracked it down and recorded it: "What makes lovemaking and reading resemble each other each other most is that within both of them times and spaces open, different from measurable time and space."

I left Miranda and Slick dancing in the hotel ballroom and went sullenly off to bed. I was lying there in a state of far too measurable time and space—faithfully but not at that time very happily married, unaccompanied and bursting with oysters—when I heard Slick's voice through the wall. He had the room next to mine. "I used to be built like a Greek god," he was saying. "Now I'm built like a god-damn Greek." That lovely woman (who thank God was *not* my destiny because she who is, is so much better, but still) made a tolerantly amused noise and I put the pillow over my head.

I have heard people justify opposition to gay marriage on the grounds of *ick* factor: they cringe at imagining what people of the same sex (pretty lesbians in some cases excepted) do in bed together. But on that basis, you wouldn't want your parents to be married. I can't think of any actual couple that I would feel right about picturing actually doing it except Elvis and Ann-Margret. Attractive people, whom I never met personally, and I don't think they'd mind.

What I am coming to, though, is that toward the end of his life, when he was struggling to stay sober, Slick e-mailed me some reflections on his life, one of which startled me. As a boy he was so pretty and delicate-featured, he wrote, that he knew from an early age he would have to make an extra effort to establish that he had, as he put it, "definite lesbian tastes."

One of Slick's jokes, to be sure, some of which were better than others, but the more I thought about it—if you looked, you could see traces of those fine features.

He had aesthetic tastes. Before his lip was smashed in a car wreck, he'd been a professional trumpet player. For years he conducted Nashville Symphony musicians at the Fourth of July picnic he helped organize. He cooked, painstakingly, great gumbo and seafood. By far the least grizzled and most sensitive portrait of Willie Nelson that I have seen is Slick's picture of him on the cover of the great album *Phases and Stages.*

Slick had romantic tastes, too, even in marriage. On January 1, 2001, when he was divorced, and his photography business was shot, and he'd alienated many of his friends, he sent me a nostalgic e-mail about New Year's Eves. Especially the one he and his wife Susan had spent, in formal attire, in a decorator friend's show window. The window display had "lots of chiffon and silver. We drank Cristal champagne, ate Krystal burgers, and had white ties on Buster and Sister." Buster was their three-legged dog and Sister their free-range cat. "We drew a strange crowd of homeless and fancy people and we never looked them in the eye."

Now, several years later, fewer people made eye contact with him. "For the last few years, I usually dressed up in a tux and went over to Sperry's [a Nashville bar] just before the ball drop. I untied my tie and let the society crowd wonder what I got invited to that they didn't. My first New Year, which I don't remember, was when I was eleven days old. I was the New Year's Baby at the Three-Mile Inn in Monroe. It is reported that I was carried around the room by Fats Waller. I guess that makes me the bouncing sixty-four-year-old continuous bar-hopper. This year my string was halted. I stayed home last night and read a book." Before the next New Year, he gave up on drying out and was found dead, at home, all dressed up to go out.

Rambling anywhere with Slick, working or playing, and it was hard to tell the difference, was like being in New Orleans. As Jelly Roll Morton said of Gypsy Shaeffer's house in Storyville, "There was everything in the line of hilarity there." Once when Slick was riding on a New Orleans riverboat, the calliope broke down. He stepped in, took the calliope apart, and fixed it. If he was, in fact, making a point of externalizing testosterone, the way he went about it was so droll and, well, I guess the expression is balls-out, that it never occurred to me that he might be compensating for the way people looked at the way he looked as a boy. Maybe Slick's dynamic derived in part from self-denial. Shades of Robert E. Lee! Except Lee was the opposite: he suppressed whatever rough and ribald side he might have had, but didn't mind looking beautiful, because his was such a Roman handsomeness. Whereas, the more I think about it, you could have boiled Slick down to a cherub.

In retrospect, though, he was, like New Orleans, a bit much. Is New Orleans overcompensating for something? Slavery, maybe, or the Duc d'Orleans's underwear? Tennessee Williams said New Orleans gave him "a kind of freedom I had always needed. And the shock of it against the Puritanism of my nature has given me a subject which I have never ceased exploiting." Maybe New Orleans is overcompensating for the rest of America.

Slick was a character. He sometimes called himself Captain America. In one of his last e-mails to me, he reported that rehab had finally convinced him he was "clinically depressed, using whiskey as an anesthetic." He hardly ever got any sleep. That's one thing he had in common with New Orleans, and with Matthew. "Until about two a.m. there's always so many people up to do things with," Slick would complain back when he was drinking and thriving and popular, "and then for another hour or so there might be somebody I could *find* who's up, to do something with, and after that I can't sleep for the stars going scritchy, scritchy, scritchy against one another." In his last years it must have been mostly Slick alone with the stars.

And I knew that, and I didn't call him up very often to see how he was doing. That time when he cried, I hugged him, which was highly unusual, and when I got back home I sent him some books and stuff, and I had him introduce me at a reading shown on C-Span once, but I think if I'd been in Slick's place and he'd been in mine, he would have done more. With lagniappe. Of course he would have been up and needing somebody to call. Who knows what anybody else's place is like?

At Slick's funeral I told his lifeguard story and our orphan-story story, and testified that on many an occasion his buoyancy had been my frog feet, which was the simple truth.

As for Matthew, he took a chip out of my shell. Could I do some small non-carnal thing for the gay community of New Orleans by way of payback? One night last year the occasion arose.

Something gay men have traditionally had in New Orleans, at all hours, is company. People opposed to gay rights used to say they didn't condemn gay people, but rather "the gay lifestyle." Now we have *Queer Eye for the Straight Guy*. But that still leaves "the gay agenda." Sounds nasty, like a frolicking secret body part. (The homophobic hymn: "Heaven protect us / From *Homo erectus*.") I asked a Republican once what exactly the gay agenda was. He looked alarmed, as if to say, "Why would *I* know?" Now it's in the open. Turns out it's weddings.

But maybe not in New Orleans. On the night of which I speak, I walked by a bar on Bourbon Street called OZ, and saw that it was jam-packed with men. The door was open, but a sign on it said, "Absolutely no video or photography equipment permitted." Notices to this effect had been posted outside a number of gay bars because, I had been told, anti-gay-agenda enthusiasts had secretly taped goings-on in some of them. (Agenda envy, maybe.) Even at a glance, I could see that there was something intense going on in OZ. Raised voices, earnest concentration. Numbers and letters being called out, as if in some sort of code. I lingered at the doorway. I saw what it was, and I was startled.

Men near the door looked up and saw me outside looking in, and my reaction. They got a good laugh out of it.

Bingo.

LAGNIAPPE WITH FRIENDS

ONE OF SLICK'S JOKES

Here's another one. A young family moved into a house next door to a vacant lot. One day a construction crew started building a house there. The young family's six-year-old daughter started chatting with the workers. She hung around and eventually the workers adopted her as a mascot. They shared their lunches with her and gave her little jobs to do to make her feel important. At the end of the first week they even presented her with a pay envelope, containing a dollar. The little girl took it home to her mother, who praised her and suggested they take it to the bank and start a savings account. When they got to the bank, the teller was equally impressed, and asked the little girl how she had come by her very own paycheck at such an early age. She proudly replied, "I've been working with a crew building a house all week."

"My goodness," said the teller, "and will you be working on the house again this week?"

"I will if those useless cocksuckers at the lumberyard ever bring us the fuckin' drywall," she replied.

THE GAY AGENDA

A rule of thumb: Beware of anyone who is not content to generalize about categories of people—hey, we all do that—but must tuck the blanket in with the definite article *the*. "The gays," "the blacks," "the liberals." Or, for that matter, "the American people." People who may have a category in common, but who otherwise vary, are thereby squeezed into capsules—we know who *they* are: *them*. And we know who *we* are: *us*. The hell we do.

TENNESSEE WILLIAMS

When he first came to the Quarter, toward the end of the thirties, you could get a dozen oysters for a quarter.

Ramble Eight:
What It Comes Down To

*Is New Orleans ever to be redeemed from its imprison-
ment in the exotic mode?*

—LEWIS P. SIMPSON

O N MONTEGUT STREET NEAR RAMPART, THERE'S
a hardy magnolia tree growing up through a rust
spot in an awning over a front porch. New Orleans gives
rise to unlikely forms of life. I mentioned Ruthie the
Duck Lady. She got to where she couldn't look after herself, and her brother Henry Junior died, and I believe so
did Pops, who kept company with her (his métier was
sticking out his extraordinarily long tongue for tips), so
she's in a home somewhere now, but every now and then
an old friend takes her out on the town, to old hangouts
like the Port o' Call or the Alpine (you'd think a bar called

the Alpine in the French Quarter would be inauthentic, but no) or the Chart Room, where they foist nonalcoholic beer on her, pretending it's Bud, because otherwise she is likely to get in the mood to knock a fellow patron right off his barstool with little or no provocation.

I don't think the lucky bead lady is in evidence much anymore either. She wore a lot of aluminum foil, to keep the aliens out, and if you declined to buy beads from her, she would curse you out in an obscure Middle-European-sounding dialect: "I have already wished for your death."

But Mr. Goodman is still out and about. He is white-bearded and wears a hardhat and an aged khaki jacket, the hat covered with fragments of lyrics of songs he says he wrote and the jacket with end-of-the-world warnings, and every time I've seen him he's been genial. Remarkably so, considering how painfully hunched his posture at a bar is, and how firmly he believes that his songs have been suppressed because he has gotten so many famous singers, whom I will not name here, pregnant.

I asked him if he was resentful, and he said, "Naaww. I was doin' what I wanted to do. You know who's behind it, don't you? Brooks and Dunn." (Big hit, "Boot-Scootin' Boogie.") He would also tell you, as early as the fall of 2001, that the government could find Osama bin Laden if it wanted to, perhaps in St. Bernard Parish: "This country has got means beyond means to find people. It keeps finding me!"

One night in the Chart Room, Mr. Goodman sold me

a lamp he had made out of a round metal ashtray, a cookie tin, the bowl of a pewter toasting cup, a bronze football, and some Mardi Gras doubloons. As lagniappe came the right to reproduce the lamp commercially in volume: "You can make your million."

I paid Mr. Goodman his price of twenty-five dollars, and for reciprocal lagniappe bought him a beer. I had a beer myself, and also bought a martini and a Manhattan for a young couple at a nearby table whose drinks I had knocked over in my eagerness to plug in the lamp and make sure it worked, which it did. In the spirit of lagniappe the Chart Room charged me, though I am not known there, only seven dollars for these four drinks. I don't think you'll get that kind of hospitality in a lap-dancing place, even in New Orleans.

Of course, though he may have taken me for someone more in the marketing line, Mr. Goodman and I are both creatives. As is Dr. Bob. There is a great deal of art in New Orleans—lots of Blue Dogs, if you go for that sort of thing, and on lower Royal, where the expensive antique shops look more stuffy than the antiques, we find the Galerie d'Art Français, with this plaque in the show window: "A Masterpiece from a Great Artist's Brush is something to which nothing that exists can be compared. However, the Pride of Possession of such works is reserved only to those who understand the importance of their existence." Just as we are about to go in and price something incomparable, we are stopped by the notice on the door: PLEASE: NO OPEN DRINK CONTAINERS. As it happens, we are carrying a beer in a go-cup, which was a New Orleans institution when Watteau was in knee pants.

Dr. Bob is a New Orleans institution whose work is widely seen there, particularly in barrooms and restaurants, where his small square signs in luminous colors on wood, with bottle-caps tacked to the frames, say "Be Nice or Leave." While roaming the Bywater, I happened upon Dr. Bob's studio, on Chartres not far from the block between Piety and Desire, across the street from a pile of bricks that used to be a macaroni factory. His is a complex of rickety structures formerly used for miscellaneous industrial storage, in which his works now abound. Signs he has found or created say "INDIAN RED's Hebrew Honky Tonk," "DR BOB's Outhouse of Blues," "SINGING CANARY's," "Hot Roasted Peanuts Parched Daily on Premises," "Mean People Produce Little Mean People," and "I'm Somewhere Near Here. Call me 905-6910, Thanks Dr. Bob, I'm Nearby."

He was there working when I walked in on him, but he didn't mind the interruption. He uses a lot of tin roofing material, and Barq's root beer caps, and zigzag strips he calls "wigglewood." He cuts snakes and alligators out of the tin: "Look at that! That's a serious alligator! That'll make your dogs bark!" He also showed me a cockroach he constructed out of a pine knot, a garbage-can lid, and a

TV antenna. And a monumental painting of his former girlfriend, nude, with big bat wings. "I miss her a lot," he said, and bat wings aside you could see why, "but she said, 'You wake up in a new world every day. I need to have a plan.' " He is not without company, though. "Little hippie girls stopped by, said they were going to squat in a warehouse over here. I said, 'But you know there's a rape and a murder in there every night?' They said, 'There is?' I said, 'Just move in over here.' They add some juice, you know? They said, 'Can we be your little elves?' I gave 'em a hundred-dollar bill and told 'em to get some food, they worked it out, you know, built that little area there that they live in. And now I can pay 'em.

"I was just fooling around here with all this and people started offering me money for it. Billionaire comes in and I say 'Don't just come in here and say, "I'll take that and that and that," you got to live with this shit,' and he says, 'No I don't.' I had to like that—if you can clean out your apartment whenever you want to. I went to New York and took my portfolio to Ivan Karp—somebody told me, 'He'll look at anything.' He pushed it away, said, 'That's the most unprofessional thing I've ever seen. You're supposed to bring slides of your work, not Polaroids of your girlfriend holding it up.' Then I found out he dealt in Warhol, Lichtenstein—people said, 'That's awesome, Ivan Karp saw your shit! And you got a rise out of him!' You know the man who invented the Nautilus had a snake farm in Slidell. He was our neighbor. 'Course I loved that, what boy wouldn't—here's a place where his lion bit me. Isn't this a great way to live?"

I bought a two-foot-by-three-foot work, a Catahoula hound cut out of ripply tin painted with spots, on a board trimmed in wigglewood and bottlecaps, for two hundred dollars, with a "Be Nice or Leave" sign for lagniappe. Dr. Bob said he would ship the big one to me. "I used to put glitter all over the packages, they said stop it because it was getting all over the delivery men, all over their shoulders and everything. I said sounds like a corporate problem to me."

A character who has proved more elusive than Dr. Bob is the Prince of Love. Joan and I were walking down upper Bourbon one moist night when a voice came from across the street: "Looking great! Lady always on the inside! You know some shit, baby." We stopped and looked as a small bearded man with dreadlocks scuttled away. A woman we didn't know stopped and said, "The person who hollered at you was the Prince of Love. Just so you'll know. He's a character in the Quotah." Then she went about her business.

A few days later I saw him, I thought, over on Royal. "Are you the one they call the Prince of Love?" I asked. He gave me the sourest look! Turns out, according to what people tell me, that he relates only to couples. He gives them blessings rooted in his voodoo beliefs. "Good luck and good sex for a whole year," he will say. "No outside sex. You can have sex outside but no outside sex. Ya got me?"

The character Joan and I have found most gratifying is not always the same person, but he's always wearing the same costume: Mr. Hand-Grenade Man, who appears around twilight every day outside a bar on Bourbon that serves a drink called the Hand Grenade, advertised as "the most powerful drink in the Quarter." The drink is an icky concoction of rum and sweet syrups, but Mr. Hand-Grenade Man is lovely. He's a pneumatic hand grenade, dark green, about nine feet tall, with a big shy smile and ingenuous bedroom eyes, and he's springy: When he dances, he jiggles up and down. If you try to pin him down as to his dynamics he will just say something muffled and grab your hand with his nose—his nose is prehensile. The only comparable union of amicability and explosiveness I can think of is the Nobel Peace Prize, founded by the man who invented dynamite. When Joan and I are in town together we try to spend a little time with Mr. Hand-Grenade Man every evening.

Am I the only one who's noticed a recurrence of triangular situations here, Nigel and the model and me and so on? I think that's because everything in New Orleans, in my experience, is a double date. When you're with a woman in New Orleans it's like being with two women, the other one being the city herself. Over the years I seem to have wound up usually with the city. And the city's man ain't me, I know that, her man is the River.

Some day, the Big One, they will be wed—Mr. Miss coming on full-commitment-strength at last into Ms. N.O., and he won't miss and she won't say no. "There will be debris flying around," an eco-catastrophe expert tells the *Times-Picayune,* "and you're going to be in the water with snakes, rodents, nutria, and fish from the lake. It's not going to be nice." Not to mention the chemical fertilizer drain-offs from Minnesota on down, and the petro-emissions from the chemical plants along what is called Cancer Alley, immediately above New Orleans. And that albino python that the priestess dances with at the Voodoo Museum. And the penguins from the Aquarium, and "Be Nice or Leave" signs and billions of Mardi Gras beads and doubloons. That flood is going to make the bottom of a gumbo pot look like a finger bowl. Shades of the Battle of New Orleans, in which the lobsterback British invaders got their lobsterbutts whipped by an ad-hoc amalgam of uniformed U.S. soldiers, polyglot pirates, old-family French Creoles, Kaintuck rivermen and free men of color—"and every man was half a horse, and half an alligator."

We'll be swept rolling and tumbling in no telling what kind of recombinance, and there's Robert E. Lee, the water up to his shoulders—does he look like he has finally found release? Nope, same noble pained expression, oh well, and we're borne out toward the great yawning Gulf, losing well-fed flesh along the way that oysters in their pearly chambers will in due time digest. But didn't we ramble.

LAGNIAPPE WITH WHAT IT COMES DOWN TO

CHARACTERS

I've never had the consistency to be a character myself, but here's the one I'd like to be. You know the balconies and courtyards of New Orleans, the high ceilings and cross-ventilation, the late hours, are all about catching a breeze. I would stand around the Quarter in a seersucker suit and a straw hat, mopping my face with a handkerchief and singing:

> *Give me a break here,*
> *The air a little movement please—*
> *Can I ever get a zephyr?*
> *I got the blues: no breeze.*

And then . . . I catch one. People see me and know it: "That's Mr. Appreciate-a-Breeze Man. They say he teaches Breeze Appreciation over by Tulane. Yep, he sho do appreciate a breeze."

OYSTERS . . . DIGEST

You can buy a T-shirt in the Quarter that has an oyster on it with eyes, a big smiley face, little hands, and arms spread wide in a welcoming gesture. "Shuck me, suck me, eat me raw," the oyster is saying. Dancing in his/her shell on a rock. Actually the gesture is more teasing than welcoming, on second thought. An ironic oyster. Maybe that's how oysters are when we're not looking.

About the Author

ROY BLOUNT JR. grew up in Georgia and lives in western Massachusetts. He is a contributing editor of *The Atlantic* and a regular panelist on National Public Radio's "Wait, Wait . . . Don't Tell Me." See royblountjr.com for details.

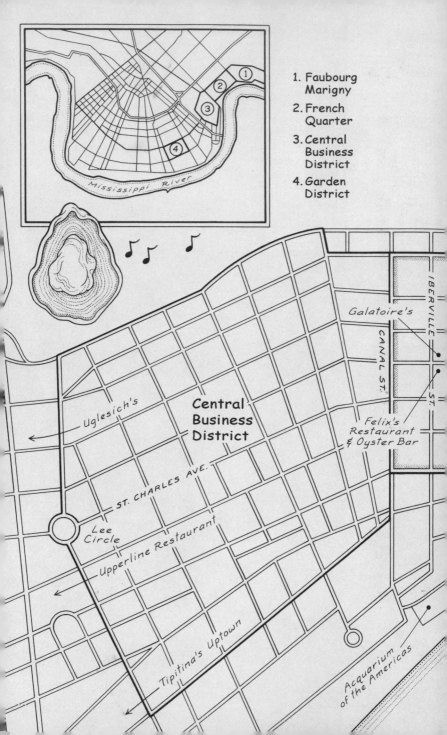

1. Faubourg Marigny
2. French Quarter
3. Central Business District
4. Garden District

Mississippi River

Galatoire's

CANAL ST.

IBERVILLE ST.

Felix's Restaurant & Oyster Bar

Uglesich's

Central Business District

ST. CHARLES AVE.

Lee Circle

Upperline Restaurant

Tipitina's Uptown

Acquarium of the Americas